Sunderland

Aspects of Local History

Glen Lyndon Dodds

Albion Press

Albion Press
40 Park Parade Roker Sunderland Tyne & Wear

ISBN 978 0 9932527 1 6

For more information on Albion Press titles email
albionpress@gmail.com

Picture credits

David John Dodds, pp. 45, 53, 67, 74, 78, 79, 81, 82.
Gavin Dodds, p. 8.
Glen Lyndon Dodds, cover, pp. 7, 32, 35, 84.
Shaun Dodds, p.15.
Derek Haynes, p. 41.
Eddie Frost, p. 47.
Local Studies Section, Sunderland City Library, p. 63.
Sunderland Antiquarian Society, pp. 23, 27, 37, 43, 55, 70.
Sunderland Echo, pp. 61, 64.

Typeset and designed by UpStyle Book Design
www.upstyledesign.co.uk

Printed and bound in Great Britain by
Mixam Printing, Unit 43, Wenta Business Centre,
Colne Way, Watford WD24 7ND

CONTENTS

Monkwearmouth
— Facets of Life in the Medieval Parish

In the late 13th century Richard de Claxton arrived at Monkwearmouth to begin his retirement. Richard was a monk. Indeed, as the former head of the region's wealthiest monastery, Durham Cathedral Priory, he had been the most important monastic figure in the North East. However, those lofty days had just come to an abrupt end for in December 1285 he was forced into retirement by someone even more exalted, Antony Bek, the imperious Bishop of Durham.

Richard, perhaps nursing a battered ego, came to Wearside to join fellow Durham monks at one of the cathedral priory's daughter houses, the cell of Monkwearmouth, which was located beside St Peter's Church. St Peter's was the place of worship not only for monks but also for the inhabitants of the substantial parish of Monkwearmouth, which included settlements as far afield as Fulwell, Southwick and Hylton.

St Peter's was much older than either the cell or parish. It was built to serve a monastic community founded in the 670s by Benedict Biscop, an aristocrat who had enthusiastically embraced the monastic ideal. By the early 1070s, though, the famous monastery he created had long since passed into history and St Peter's, which had doubtless become a parish church in the interim, was derelict as a result of recent destruction caused by a Scottish army.

In the mid-1070s, however, a small band of monks, inspired by Monkwearmouth's former greatness, arrived on the scene and restored the site where monastic life thus resumed. But less than a decade later, in 1083, William de St Calais, the Bishop of Durham, transferred the monks (and others resident at Jarrow) to Durham, where he was founding a Benedictine priory. As part of the new monastery's endowment, he granted the priory the parish of Monkwearmouth.

It is often said that after Durham Cathedral Priory was founded some monks continued to reside at Monkwearmouth and Jarrow where they manned daughter houses of the new monastery. Cells undoubtedly existed at both locations during the Middle Ages. Nevertheless, Alan Piper aptly comments: 'It is not until the Statutes drawn up by the Prior of Durham in 1235 that there is a clear indication that they were numbered among Durham's cells, and so the documentary evidence will allow no firmer statement than that the cells of Jarrow and Wearmouth had been established by 1235.'[1]

Some masters of the cell at Monkwearmouth had previously held positions in Durham Priory's administration. For example, Alan de Marton, the cell's head in the years 1335-38, had among other things acted as the bursar and terrar, key roles in the management of the priory's large and far-flung estate. Sometimes the masters had two fellow monks under their charge, but often there was only one other monk. Personnel changed on a frequent basis and few monks spent several years at Monkwearmouth.

In general Benedictine monks, unlike members of some monastic orders, did not serve a pastoral role in parishes owned by their monasteries. Consequently, at St Peter's a chaplain was employed to care for the spiritual needs of the parishioners.

The main buildings of the cell were located to the south of St Peter's, which underwent extension and rebuilding during the course of the Middle Ages—for one thing, the nave was enlarged, most likely in the 13th century, by the construction of a north aisle—and the small monastic complex included a cloister. In 1321 and thereafter, it was recorded that the cell possessed a master's chamber, as well as a hall, kitchen, bakehouse and pantry. Among other structures were a brewhouse and granary, and there was also a courtyard.

At Monkwearmouth the monks ran a demesne (home farm) which comprised at least 120 acres. The farm was run by using paid employees and labour of tenants from the village of Monkwearmouth, a township granted to the cell by the priory. In 1360 livestock included 13 oxen, two milking cows, 102 sheep, 52 lambs, 50 pigs, 21 geese, one cock and four hens. At other times, capons (cocks castrated to improve the quality of their flesh for consumption) are also listed. Arable farming also occurred and usually approximately 80 to 90 acres were under culti-

1 A.J. Piper, *Durham Monks at Wearmouth*, 1974, p. 2.

St Peter's Church, Monkwearmouth

vation. Wheat, barley, peas and beans were the main crops. In 1360, for instance, 29 acres were sown with wheat, 21 with barley, one acre with mixed corn, whereas 60 acres grew beans and peas.

Additional sources of income for the cell included payments for burial at St Peter's Church and rents from the residents of the village of Monkwearmouth. Money was also obtained from a ferry. This crossed the River Wear close to the church and operated between Monkwearmouth and the small borough of Sunderland which belonged to the Bishop of Durham and was founded in the 12th century. Until a great flood occurred in 1400, it was possible, though, for pedestrians to cross the river mouth at low tide instead.

Tithes were another source of revenue and the garbal tithes (a tenth of the corn harvest) were the most important. A proportion of the grain was consumed by the monks and their staff and was also used as animal fodder. But the corn was also sold. For example, Ben Dodds notes that

A 13th-century doorway at St Peter's Church

the cell's head dealt with 'some of his tithe wheat and barley in 1386-7' in this way 'but kept the rest back because it could only be sold at a low price.'[1]

For most of its existence the cell only received corn tithes from Monkwearmouth and Fulwell. The grain tithes of Hylton and Southwick were usually dealt with by Durham's bursar and this was also the case with two settlements in the parish, Newton, part of the Hylton estate, and Threptend (whose location is uncertain) mentioned in the 14th century. At times, the grain was kept in hand by the bursar and so, after being threshed and winnowed, was transported to Durham where, for instance, the monastic community required large quantities of wheat to make bread. However, the tithes were often sold instead just before the harvest. On this point Dodds comments: 'Given that the amount paid for the tithe was negotiated prior to the harvest, the purchaser must have been reliant on the previous years' prices in his

1 Dodds, Ben, (2002), *Tithe and agrarian output between the Tyne and Tees, 1350-1450*, Durham theses, Durham University. Available at Durham E-Theses online: http://etheses.dur.ac.uk/4191/, p. 67.

estimation of the likely sale value of the tithe crops.'[1] Buyers were often local men like John Reid of Southwick who, according to a rental of 1381/2, acquired the tithes of that township.

The Villages and their Residents

The village of Monkwearmouth was centred on a large green and lay on elevated ground a short distance northwest of St Peter's Church. The settlement occupied land extending eastward from today's Wheatsheaf public house to the line of present day North Church Street. Fulwell, on the other hand, which likewise had a green, lay on the line of what is now Station Road whereas Southwick's dwellings faced a green that has survived (in modified form) to the present day. Hylton, of which less is known, was situated a couple of minutes' walk to the northwest of the residence of the most exalted parishioners, the baronial Hylton family. In addition, well upstream from St Peter's, there may have been a hamlet at what became North Hylton, a place where there were two crossings of the river, a ford and, from at least the early 1320s onward, a sturdy ferry capable of transporting cattle across the Wear.

The tenants of the villages mentioned, with the exception of Hylton, held their land from the monks of Durham Priory to whom Monkwearmouth and Southwick were granted in 1083, as was likely also true of Fulwell. The latter was certainly owned by the monks from at least the mid 12th century.

In the early 13th century, for example, tenants of the priory included William of Fulwell to whom Thomas Melsonby, the Prior of Durham in the years 1234-44, granted a toft (enclosure for a dwelling) and 18 acres of land at Southwick. The previous tenant had been a fisherman named Gilbert who derived part of his livelihood by catching salmon at Ebbeyare (one of several fisheries that existed in the River Wear at Southwick during the Middle Ages) where the fish were caught as the tide ebbed.

For much of the medieval period, in addition to working land they held for the benefit of themselves and their families, some tenants and

---

1 Dodds B., (2002), *'Durham Priory tithes and the Black Death between Tyne and Tees'*, Northern History 39 (1), March 2002, p. 12.

especially the holders of bondlands (of which there were ten at Southwick, each comprising 48 acres), were obligated to work for a specified number of days per week on their lord's demesne. This was part of the estate the lord kept in hand and farmed directly using paid labour and the service of tenants, and within the parish there were demesnes at Monkwearmouth, Fulwell and Hylton.[1] In addition, the holders of bondlands, and indeed all customary tenants—those who were not freeholders—were required to perform various tasks at harvesttime.

Freeholders, of course, enjoyed higher social status but even they were expected to render some labour services. Alisdair Dobie cites the case of one such at Southwick mentioned in a bursar's rent-roll of 1270. In return for his holding, the tenant 'owed military service, suit in the free court of the prior, nine pence to the terrar for cornage, five hens to the cellarer, a day of ploughing and harrowing, three days of weeding, and four days of reaping with a single man at the manor of Fulwell, and finally seven shillings and fourpence to be paid there to the bursar.'[2] Within the parish (as elsewhere) freeholders were a small minority. Indeed, of the tenants mentioned in a priory rental of 1340-1 only four had that status.

This rental names 19 tenants at Monkwearmouth, four of whom each held a toft (enclosure for a dwelling) and 48 acres of land, as was true for example of the freeholders Reginald of Wearmouth and Robert de Castro. The majority of their neighbours held much smaller holdings of 12 and 16 acres or thereabouts. Margery of Southwick had an even smaller stake in the community, namely a toft and one acre. Thomas, son of Adam, merely had a cottage.

The most important person in the parish mentioned in the rental

---

1 At times the monks of Durham leased certain demesnes rather than manage them directly. Richard Lomas has shown that this was true of the demesne at Fulwell for 'in the years before 1325...all available evidence indicates that it was leased.' R. Lomas. 'The Priory of Durham and its Demesnes in the Fourteenth and Fifteenth Centuries', *The Economic History Review* second series vol. XXXI, No. 3., 1978, p. 341.

2 Dobie, Alisdair John (2011), *Accounting, Management and Control at Durham Cathedral Priory, c. 1250-c.1420,* Durham Theses, Durham University. Available at Durham E-Theses online, http://etheses.dur.ac.uk/609/, p. 63. Incidentally, freeholders often ignored the obligation of attending the prior's free court (which met frequently each year) and were fined as a result.

was John of Hedworth, who had 100 acres of freehold land at Southwick. Hedworth, who had been born into a leading family in the parish of Jarrow—which likewise belonged to Durham Priory—was also the lessee of a fishery in the River Wear and of Southwick mill. Richard Ayre, Southwick's other freeholder at this date, held 63 acres. At the opposite end of the scale were tenants like John, son of Radulph, who held a toft and six acres. The holders of Southwick's ten bondlands are not listed in the rental because they only performed labour services.

The same source names eight tenants at Fulwell and records that the two largest holdings there each contained 32 acres whereas three other tenants each held 16 acres, as was true of Simon of Moorsley who evidently came from the township of that name in the parish of Houghton-le-Spring. Other tenants included Patrick of Wearmouth. He simply held a toft but no land. In addition, several holdings at Fulwell were not held in return for a money rent and so their tenants do not appear in the rental.

Sadly, a high proportion of people in the parish of Monkwearmouth died wretchedly a few years later when the Black Death struck Wearside in the summer of 1349. Evidence indicates that in County Durham as a whole over 50 per cent of the population lost their life, and mortality here was of comparable magnitude for Durham's monks recorded that four of their tenants died at Fulwell, and eight and eleven at Southwick and Monkwearmouth respectively.

Following the plague, owing to the drop in population, it became commonplace for tenants two have more than one holding. Furthermore, Durham Priory increasingly dispensed with labour services on its badly hit estate in favour of receiving money from tenants instead. In the early 1350s, for instance, labour services were replaced by money rents for six holdings at Fulwell, and by 1384 Southwick's bondlands were all let.

What is more, by the latter date the priory had begun to change the length of tenure. Hitherto, at least in the third quarter of the 14th century, tenants mostly entered holdings for life. Now tenancies for periods of years were coming into play. Richard Lomas cites the example of William, son of Adam. In the summer of 1389 he commenced a six year tenancy of two holdings at Fulwell, the first recorded case of land held there on such terms.[1] During the 1390s, short leases became the norm on the priory's estate and 'short-leasehold tenure was accompanied by an increase in the tempo of the land market, which suggests that the tenants saw in the short lease the means of liberation from irksome and long resented constraints on their freedom to deal in land.'[2]

Evidence from the halmote courts

The lives of the majority of the parishioners were regulated by halmote courts held by officers of the Prior of Durham. These courts sat on a regular basis, several months apart, and were presided over by two very important members of the monastic community, Durham's terrar and bursar, and a lay colleague, the prior's steward, a member of the gentry.

The court usually met at Fulwell and Monkwearmouth and dealt with a variety of matters. For example at a halmote in the autumn of 1296, William, the son of Patrick, became the holder of a toft and land at Monkwearmouth which Adam, the son of Alice, previously held. In return, William would pay a rent of 17s. 4d. per annum and was also required, *inter alia*, to perform customary services. Of Fulwell, the same halmote noted that the lands of the blacksmith were currently in the hands of the Prior of Durham and that Thomas, the son of Michael, became the tenant of a toft and land for which he would perform the services due from the tenancy and pay the prior 20s. Furthermore, several tenants at Southwick, including William Etteben and John Ross, were fined for sowing land without authorisation and, again, tenancies changed hands. We also read that Alexander of Southwick gave half a mark to the monks of Durham so that his daughter could be permitted to marry.

In early 1370 a halmote ordered the tenants of Fulwell, Monkwearmouth and Southwick to have their grain ground at the prior's mill in the latter township and not elsewhere[3] and this was the normal

1 Lomas, Richard Arthur (1973), *Durham Cathedral Priory as a Landowner and a Landlord 1290-1540*, Durham Theses, Durham University. Available at Durham E-Theses online: http://etheses.dur.ac.uk/8057/, p. 42.

2 R. Lomas, 'Developments in Land Tenure on the Prior of Durham's Estate in the Later Middle Ages', *Northern History*, vol. XIII, 1977, p. 39.

3 *'Fulwell. Injunctum est omnibus tenentibus istius villae et villat' de Wermouth et Suthwyk quod molant ad molend' de Suthwyk et non alibi.'* W.H. Longstaffe & J. Booth (eds.), *Halmota Prioratus Dunelmensis*, Surtees Society volume lxxxii, 1889, p. 85. The halmote in question was the third and final one of a series begun the previous summer.

state of affairs. For using the mill, the tenants were charged a multure (percentage of the milled flour) and both freeholders and customary tenants paid the same amount, normally one measure in 13.

Southwick's mill was undoubtedly the most important within the parish and at this date may well have been water-powered, as would have been the case for generations. During the course of the 14th century, however, watermills in Durham were gradually replaced or supplemented by windmills. These were present from at least the opening decade of the century and this development also affected the parish of Monkwearmouth. In the summer of 1383, for example, the records of Durham Priory mention a windmill (*molendinum ventriticum*) at Southwick.[1] Presumably, it was located on the high ground lying just to the northwest of the village green where a windmill existed in more recent times. The priory let the mill and for several years in the early 15th century the lessee was a bigwig in the parish, Thomas Egermond of Fulwell, evidently an enterprising figure and the most important tenant at Fulwell by the mid 1390s.

Halmotes also dealt with cases of immorality. In some instances, the offences were not repeated (or at least did not come to light again) but this was not always the case. Indeed, Agnes Hoby of Southwick and Matilda Creler of Monkwearmouth were notable repeat offenders. Lomas mentions that they were fined 'fifteen and twelve times respectively between 1375 and 1396' and thus 'wonders if they were adding to their income or indulging their appetites or both.'[2] Whatever the truth, both women, like the vast majority of the inhabitants of the parish, belonged to the lower orders of society. This, however, was emphatically not true of the Hyltons (or Hiltons), the most important family in the neighbourhood.

The Hyltons before 1400

Fanciful accounts of the family's history mention the exploits of characters such as Adam Hylton and Lancelot Hylton who are said, respectively, to have flourished in the days of King Athelstan in the early 10th

---

1 *Ibid.*, p. 177.

2 Lomas, Richard Arthur (1973), *Durham Cathedral Priory as a Landowner and a Landlord*, p. 56.

century and at the time of the Norman Conquest. What is certain is that the Hyltons held their estate by 1135 at the latest, as is evident from information submitted by Bishop Hugh du Puiset of Durham to Henry II in 1166. By the latter date, moreover, the Hyltons were allowed to have their own chaplain but had to attend St Peter's Church for the great festivals of the Christian calendar such as Christmas and Easter and were required to provide various dues to the parish church as well.

In the first half of the 13th century, Sir Alexander de Hylton granted three marks a year (revenue from his mill at Hylton) to St Peter's. The money was bequeathed to support a chaplain who would celebrate mass in the church at an altar dedicated to St Laurence. He would do so for the souls of Alexander, his forbears and descendants. The grant is undated but occurred before the end of the priorate of Ralph Kerneth of Durham who died in 1234, for in connection with the bequest the prior referred to Alexander as 'our venerable friend.'[1]

Whereas the majority of the inhabitants of the parish will have spent most of their lives within its boundaries, the Hyltons were cosmopolitan figures who often ventured further afield. Alexander, who would have been bilingual (French was the language of polite society) is a case in point. Through his mother he had inherited land in Northumberland—Shilbottle, Guyzance and Rennington—to which he devoted some of his time. Moreover he married Agnes de Verly, a Yorkshire heiress whose family was based at Swine in Holderness.[2] In early 1241 Alexander left England for the Holy Land in the company of the Earl of Albermarle and other men of rank, a daunting enterprise from which he never returned for he died abroad the following year, leaving an under-age son in England.

In the years around 1400 one of Alexander's descendants, Sir William Hylton, who was born at Alnwick Castle in Northumberland in 1355—*fuit natus in castro de Alnewyk in comitatu de Northumbr'*[3]— replaced his

---

1 *Venerabilis amicus noster Alexander de Helton.* Quoted by W.H. Longstaffe in 'The Church of Guyzance', *Archaeologia Aeliana* , new series volume iii, 1859, p. 135.

2 In 1288 Alexander's son and successor Robert, who fought against Henry III in the Barons' War, granted Swine to one of his younger sons.

3 H.A. Doubleday and Lord Howard de Walden (eds.), *The Complete Peerage*, vol. vii, 1929, p. 25.

Hylton Castle viewed from the west

ancestral seat at Hylton with a sophisticated castle, complete with a magnificent heraldic display on the imposing façade that proclaimed his links with other members of high society.

William, a martial figure, fought against the Scots and French and, on 16 April 1386, was granted 50 marks per annum by Richard II to serve the king in peace and war with 20 men-at-arms and 20 archers. Subsequently, though, in 1399 Hylton evidently ranked among those who took up arms against the monarch, an increasingly tyrannical figure. Richard was captured and overthrown by his cousin the Duke of Lancaster who thus became Henry IV and, at Westminster on 23 October, as a contemporary parliamentary roll states, '*Le Baron de Hilton*' was one of 58 lords who consented to Richard's permanent incarceration.[1]

1 I have discussed the Hyltons and their castle at greater length in *A History of Sunderland* (third edition), 2011, pp. 46-51.

The 15th century & Beyond

By the start of the 15th century most of the demesne land of Durham Priory was no longer exploited directly by the monastic community—the rising cost of labour was a contributory factor—and demesnes were leased instead. In some cases this arrangement was of long standing, but the policy of abandoning direct management gained momentum as the 14th century drew to a close. Consequently, most of the demesnes controlled by the bursar were let. Nevertheless, at Fulwell (likewise the bursar's responsibility) the demesne was 'still in hand' when the new century began and had been so for most of the 1300s. However, in 1416, it too was finally leased on what proved to be a permanent basis and, from 1418 onward, the tenant of the manor was almost invariably a member of the Wake family of Southwick.

The bursar was not responsible for the demesne at Monkwearmouth, which was controlled by the monastic cell. Here, in harmony with the general trend, there was a shift—albeit modest in scale—away from direct exploitation for several acres of the demesne were rented out for some years in the late 14th century and a larger proportion in the early 15th. Nevertheless, as Piper comments: 'The appearance of harvesting expenses on virtually every surviving account shows that the monks engaged in direct management of some arable land throughout the last two centuries of the cell's existence.'[1]

Turning to other matters, in the summer of 1419 William, the aforementioned head of the Hylton family, was welcomed into the fraternity of Durham Cathedral Priory by the head of the monastic community, Prior John Washington. So, too, was Hylton's wife Dionisia—the daughter of Sir Robert Hylton of Swine, the head of a junior branch of the line. This was not an honour Durham's monks bestowed freely and doubtless reflects Washington's desire to be on friendly terms with one of the leading families in the county.

Relations between the Hyltons and the monks of Durham were, in fact, sometimes far from friendly owing to disputes on such matters as the non-attendance of the family at St Peter's and squabbles over various dues they owed to the monks. Matters came to a head in March 1439, four

---

1 Piper, *Durham Monks at Wearmouth*, p. 4.

Hylton Castle from the south

years after William was succeeded as head of the family by his son, Sir Robert. Animosity reached such a pitch that Robert's own son and heir William burst into the church 'wt outyn ony prayer or reuerence [reverence] theer made or shewid to ye blessid sacrament', and swore a great oath that there was nothing to stop him from pulling one of the monks out of the cell and sending him to Durham with 'his feete [bound] undre a horse baly.' In addition, Hylton laid hands on William Lyham, the master of the cell, and contemptuously asked him 'Whoo was yi sire?' 'Who indeed?', asks the historian Richard Dobson. He continues: 'As in the case of nearly all fifteenth-century monks of Durham, the question cannot be answered at all precisely; but it is clear enough that he is unlikely to have been a person with whom members of the Hilton family would ever have spent the time of day.'[1] The situation became so threatening that Lyham was permitted to leave Monkwearmouth by the Prior of Durham because he feared to remain. Moreover, in 1459 during another dispute between the Hyltons and the priory, the

1 J. Raine (ed.), *The Inventories and Account Rolls of the Benedictine Houses or Cells of Jarrow and Monkwearmouth in the County of Durham,* Surtees Society vol. xxix,1854, p. 241; R.B. Dobson, *Church and Society in the Medieval North of England*, 1996, p. 60. William Hylton's mother was a granddaughter of a very prominent figure, Thomas Beauchamp, the 11th Earl of Warwick, a distinguished soldier (he was one of the first Knights of the Garter) whose vast possessions included Barnard Castle in County Durham.

family's chaplain, Robert Stainton, was excommunicated by the monks of Monkwearmouth who accused him of misappropriating tithes.

It will be recalled that the monastic cell derived income from a ferry that crossed the river between Monkwearmouth and Sunderland. In the 15th century, though, the monks' right to the ferry and its revenue were challenged. What is more, the monks themselves were charged for using the ferry by Robert Jackson who had leased the borough of Sunderland from the Bishop of Durham.

Hence in 1437 detailed arguments were put forward on the cell's behalf by the Prior of Durham, John Washington. Among other things, he argued that the financial accounts (*compoti*) of the masters of the cell dating back over a century clearly showed that the monks had operated the ferry since at least 1335 when Alan de Marton was the cell's head.[1] Nevertheless, the master's accounts for the following year contain a forlorn entry noting that the cell had received no income from the ferry that year. Of the dispute's ultimate outcome, we read that 'it appears to have been the bishop who triumphed, for he included the ferryboat and the right of passage across the Wear in later grants of the borough of Sunderland.'[2]

In the early 15th century the cell's fortunes were at a low ebb and it was often in debt. To help matters, in 1425 the corn-tithes of Southwick and Hylton were granted to the master. In Southwick's case this was a temporary measure, for the tithes returned to the bursar's control in 1434. Income from corn tithes was however less than had been the case in previous generations for the amount of land under cultivation had fallen largely due to a smaller population and greater emphasis on pastoral farming. Indeed, in some townships the fields were not sown and the parish of Monkwearmouth was no exception. The accounts of the masters of the cell, for example, show that in the late 1420s and early years of the following decade no tithes were received from Hylton. No tithes were also received from the township in 1437, although on this

---

1 *ut patet expresse in diversis compotis dictorum magistrorum ... videlicet de anno domini millesimo cccxxxv in statu alani de marton.* Quoted from Dobie, *Accounting, Management and Control at Durham Cathedral Priory,* p. 143.

2 G. Cookson (ed.), *Victoria County History* of *Durham vol. 5, Sunderland,* 2015, p. 52.

occasion the reason was that the tithes were once again in the hands of the bursar, albeit a temporary measure.

Returning to events at Fulwell, by 1440 the customary land was held by three tenants, namely Thomas Nicholson junior (81 acres), Nicholas Ayre (64 acres) and Robert Watson, (46 acres). Ayre was still holding his tenancy in 1470—which had been renewed on several occasions—when a new arrangement came into effect. The township's land, including the demesne, was divided between a four-strong syndicate. Ayre was one of the members. So, too, was Thomas Lambert, hitherto lessee of the 81-acre block of holdings. The syndicate also included a newcomer from nearby Cleadon, William Mathow. The syndicate's fourth member, Robert Wake, was no stranger to Fulwell for in the years before the formation of the syndicate he was a lessee of the manor's demesne land.[1] 'According to the terms of the new lease', states Lomas, 'each man took a quarter of the township and its land plus a quarter of the manor with its land and meadow but minus the stock which was returned to the lord. The rent of each share was £5. 8s. 6d. (£2. 5s. 2d. for the township, £3. 3s. 4d. for the manor) payable to the Bursar plus 16s. 8d. to the Master of Wearmouth in lieu of garb tithe. After 1470 the only changes were ones of personnel, although the Mathow family was still holding its share in 1539.'[2] Elsewhere in the parish syndication occurred, for before 1491 a four-strong syndicate was formed at Monkwearmouth and by the early 1520s (if not earlier) customary land at Southwick was likewise leased out, in this case to a syndicate of three men.

Southwick's mill continued to play a role in the lives of the priory's tenants. Halmote records dating from 1505-06 mention, among other things, that the miller was 'prosecuted by a Fulwell tenant for theft' and that the tenants of Monkwearmouth and Fulwell 'had to be reminded of their obligation to grind at Southwick, and one member of the latter

---

1 Richard Lomas, in 'The Priory of Durham and its Demesnes' cited earlier, states that the manor was always let to a single tenant between 1416 and 1470. However, an inventory of 1464 records that at that time it was let 'to Robert Wake and others' for a term of 15 years, nine of which had passed. W. Greenwell (ed.), *Feodarium Prioratus Dunelmensis: a Survey of the Estates of the Prior and Convent of Durham, compiled in the 15th century*, Surtees Society, vol. lviii, 1872, p. 120.

2 Lomas, *Durham Cathedral Priory as a Landowner*, p. 45.

community was amerced [fined] for not doing so.'[1] Contrary to past practice, however, the priory's tenants could use querns to grind corn but only if a licence had been purchased from the mill's lessee.

Arable farming was still undertaken in the parish on a fairly significant scale. In 1533, for instance, the corn tithes of Southwick totalled 18 quarters of wheat, 12 quarters and one bushel of barley, four and a half quarters of peas and beans, and five quarters of oats. Southwick's corn tithes at this date were kept in hand by the bursar.

When the residents of the parish harvested their crops that year and Durham's bursar carried out his duties as usual, England was on the eve of momentous change. Much against the pope's wishes, Henry VIII (who had ruled the country since 1509) had set aside his first wife Catherine of Aragon in order to marry Anne Boleyn, and the king's strong anti-papal sentiment now led to the legislation of the Reformation Parliament. In early 1536, for example, a law was enacted that resulted in the nationwide closure of small monastic communities, including the cell of Monkwearmouth. What is more, the greater religious houses soon experienced the same fate. At Durham, the end came on 31 December 1539 when the cathedral priory was closed down. Hence, as a result of the Dissolution of the Monasteries, monks no longer loomed large in the lives of the residents of the parish of Monkwearmouth. An era had passed.

---

1 R. Lomas, 'The Black Death in County Durham', *Journal of Medieval History* 15, (1989), p. 136.

FORD TOWNSHIP — A BRIEF ANALYSIS OF THE POPULATION IN 1851

During the course of the 19th century Wearside witnessed a population explosion and Ford township, which covered 1,029 acres, was no exception. In 1801, at the time of the first national census, it had 602 inhabitants but by 1831 the figure had climbed to 911. Much faster growth ensued during the 1830s—the most significant decade for population growth of the entire century on Wearside as a whole. Consequently, by 1841 the population of the township had soared to 1,720. More modest expansion occurred thereafter and by 1851 the figure had climbed to 1,913.

Primarily, growth happened as a result of the arrival of migrants who came to seek employment in local industries which included shipbuilding, the manufacture of pottery and the production of copperas and paper. Some of the industries were already present at the start of the 19th century but others were of recent date, as was true of papermaking for the Ford Paper Mill (located less than a mile downriver of South Hylton, the main centre of population) opened in 1838.

Although the overwhelming majority of the township's inhabitants were working class, others led much more comfortable lives. This was certainly true of the residents of Ford Hall, a mansion erected in 1785 in the southeast part of the township and which stood in wooded grounds in a secluded location well away from the riverside. In 1851 it was the home of a 37-year-old widower named William Hay, a timber merchant who had been born in Monkwearmouth. He shared the residence with his mother-in-law, Ann Elizabeth Alexander, and sister-in-law, Sophia Louisa Alexander, respectively born at Jarrow and Bishopwearmouth. Also present was his nephew, Charles Douglas Alexander, aged 7, a British subject born in East India, and a 5-year-old niece called Helen Louisa Alexander who had come into the world in Bishopwearmouth.

Interestingly, the servants at Ford Hall in 1851 also came from far and wide. Agnes Huic, the 20-year-old governess, had been born in Edinburgh whereas the housekeeper's birthplace was Newcastle. The nurse came from Waldridge in County Durham and the cook was a British subject born in West India. In addition, the housemaid's place of birth was Newcastle whilst the kitchen maid and two house servants were born in Yorkshire. That county was also the place of origin of the 30-year-old coachman, Thomas Raw, who lived in Ford Hall Cottage.

Many other inhabitants of the township also came from far afield. In 1851, for example, 110 people, almost 6 per cent of the population, had been born in Ireland, as was true of a 68-year-old shipwright named Alexander Hepburn who resided at Ford Dock Yard House but had been born at Kilkenny. Another Irishman was 23-year-old John O'Connor, also a shipwright, whose wife Sarah (two years his junior) had likewise been born across the Irish Sea. The couple lived in Waterside Row and had a one-year-old son born locally.

Large numbers of Irish migrants arrived in England as a result of the Great Famine that began in 1845. In Ford's case, though, the township had already attracted significant Irish settlement for the census of 1841 records the presence of 113 people of Irish birth, some of whom worked at the paper mill.

Ten years later, the township also had a fairly strong contingent of residents from north of the border. One such was Robert Forbes, a 24-year-old who had first seen the light of day at Stromness in the Orkney Isles. However, Scots were less numerous than their counterparts from Ireland for they totalled 63, just over 3 per cent of the population.

Other residents, of course, came from far-flung places in England. Charlotte Brown, a 26-year-old housemaid at Claxheugh Cottages, is a case in point for she was born at Kingston-upon-Thames in Surrey. Another example is Mary Harker, aged 66, whose birthplace was Sheerness in Kent. Mary lived in Church Street and was the wife of a farm labourer.

A substantial number of Ford's residents were born in Newcastle upon Tyne and Northumberland. All told, this was true of 155 inhabitants whose places of birth included Alnwick, Berwick upon Tweed, Hexham and Holy Island. Not surprisingly, though, more came from Newcastle

Ford Hall

than any other place between the Tyne and Tweed. In fact, 50 were born in the regional capital.

Among migrants from north of the Tyne were 50-year-old William Davison, a 'farm servant' working at South Ford Farm, who had been born at Rothbury. His wife, Sarah, also aged 50, likewise came from Northumberland for her place of birth was Felton, whilst their 19-year-old daughter Mary Ann was a dressmaker who had first set eyes on the world at Rennington in Northumberland. Moreover, in Church Street lived the Longridge family whose head, 52-year-old William, was a potter born at Newburn. His wife, two years his junior, was born at Liverpool but Newcastle was the birthplace of their three sons, aged 12 to 20, two of whom, George and William, worked as shipwrights.

Understandably, the largest category of migrants was comprised of people born in County Durham. This was true of William Trotter, aged 40, who was employed as the manager of Ford Pottery. Stanhope, in Weardale, was his place of birth, as was also the case with his sister Phebe, a housekeeper. Several other residents of the township hailed from Stanhope and other distant parts of the county. But most of the newcomers came from much closer to home. For example, 17 had been born in Houghton-le-Spring and 14 in Southwick, whereas 30 were born in Monkwearmouth. One such was George Chambers, a 47-year-old potter (one of the residents of Ford Gill Houses) whose wife, Elizabeth, was aged 44 and whose life had begun at St John's Chapel in upper Weardale. The couple had six children. Their eldest child, Elizabeth, was a 16-year-old dressmaker born in Bishopwearmouth, but the other offspring were all born in South Hylton.

The above gives an indication of the diverse nature of Ford's population in the 19th century and the same was also true of other townships on Wearside for large numbers of people flocked here to find work in the shipyards and other sources of employment.

In 1855 it was observed in *Sketches of Public Men of the North*, that 'For all practical purposes, Sunderland is as new as an Australian or Yankee settlement.' The same could aptly have been said of Ford township.

A YANKEE SETTLEMENT — ASPECTS OF SUNDERLAND'S HISTORY BETWEEN 1831 & 1881

In late 1831 Asiatic Cholera made its deadly presence felt in Sunderland. The port was, in fact, the point of entry for the first outbreak of the disease in the nation's history and the first deaths probably occurred in August. What is certain is that on 7 November, at the behest of the Privy Council in London, a 15-day quarantine was imposed on all vessels leaving the River Wear. This measure harmed the export trade, a central facet of the local economy, and was strongly resented by Wearsiders of all classes, especially as travel by road was not likewise restricted.

Feelings rans so high that local medical men who said that Asiatic Cholera was present were subjected to strong criticism and pressure. At a public meeting held on 11 November at the Exchange, which had opened in 1814 and served as Sunderland's commercial and administrative centre, members of the community decided that the cases of cholera were merely severe examples of bowel complaints! Furthermore, a resolution drawn up on the 12th and signed by many local physicians and surgeons, declared, among other things, that the disease had not been imported to Wearside and was not contagious.

Miserable weeks ensued. In fact the cholera epidemic lasted into the opening months of 1832 (by which time it had spread to Newcastle upon Tyne and elsewhere) and claimed a total of 215 lives in Sunderland and its immediate neighbours such as Bishopwearmouth.

Most of those struck down by cholera on Wearside lived in the overcrowded and unsanitary parish of Sunderland, whose population numbered around 17,000. Of that area, Dr Barry observed in a letter penned at the time of the outbreak: 'Sunderland contains almost exclusively the working poor, with their parents, wives, and children, many of whom disease and age renders incapable of earning their own subsistence. They live in crowded dwellings and are most strikingly disproportionate in numbers to those capable of paying parish rates.'[1]

Neighbouring Bishopwearmouth, whose population numbered some 14,500 people in 1831, was generally more appealing and the most upmarket houses were found in Fawcett Street, which had begun to be developed a decade or so earlier. The street, which was residential in character, was partly lined with homes of the well-to-do and the process of building further homes along the imposing street was not yet complete and would continue into the 1840s.

By 1851 Sunderland's population numbered almost 64,000—the 1830s had witnessed particularly fast growth—and further increase followed. As a consequence, by 1881 the town (whose boundary had been extended in 1867) had a population that exceeded 116,500.

By this date the desirability of Fawcett Street as a residential area had been undermined—for one thing, an increasing number of homes had been transformed into offices for professional figures such as lawyers—and instead prosperous families now favoured the Ashbrooke area, a short distance south of the town centre. Some of the homes there were substantial detached residences like Ashbrooke Hall, an Italianate villa built in 1864 to serve as an imposing and sumptuous residence for James Hartley, the well-known glassmaker. More numerous, though, were terraced properties and some of these, such as the Esplanade (built in 1853-65) were private streets with gates to limit access.

Some of Sunderland's working class, on the other hand, lived in modern cottages 'occupied by one or at most by two families' and were 'comfortable and cleanly'; whereas less fortunate families shared tenements of three storeys or more with 'only a single room for each family, ranging from 12 feet by 8 feet to 14 feet by 10 feet.' Moreover, such dwellings were badly ventilated 'partly on account of the houses being built in rows back to back, without any passages or yards between them.'[2]

In late 1849, Robert Rawlinson visited Sunderland on behalf of the government and his report duly appeared in 1851. Among other things,

---

1 Quoted in S.T. Miller, *The Book of Sunderland*, 1989, p. 58.

2 D.B. Reid, *Report on the Sanitary Condition of Newcastle, Gateshead, North Shields, Sunderland, Durham and Carlisle—Appendix to Second Report*, 1845, p.192.

The Cedars in 1867

Rawlinson mentions the presence of 'many narrow streets, filled with the poorest inhabitants, having no proper conveniences, but living in filth, and ever breathing an atmosphere loaded with the seeds of disease.'[1]

Of Bishopwearmouth, Rawlinson observed, it 'is much more regularly

1 R. Rawlinson, *Report to the General Board of Health on a Preliminary Inquiry as to the Sewerage, Drainage, Supply of Water and the Sanitary Condition of the Borough of Sunderland in the County of Durham*, 1851, p. 23.

laid out than the old parts of Sunderland, and there are some streets of better class houses; but even here, for want of the necessary local power, streets are undrained and unpaved, and many of them must remain so under the present divided authority.'[1]

The town council, established under the Municipal Corporations Act of 1835, certainly did not enjoy a monopoly on local government. In 1851, though, matters improved for its authority was greatly extended. Powers of other local bodies, such as the Sunderland and Bishopwearmouth Improvement Commissions (both established in 1810 and empowered to pave, light and clean the streets etc) were vested in the corporation by Act of Parliament.

Politics

As a result of the Reform Act of 1832, Sunderland was granted the right to elect its own MPs and a two-seater constituency was created. This contained the parish of Sunderland and also embraced Bishopwearmouth and other neighbouring communities, namely Bishopwearmouth Panns, Monkwearmouth, Monkwearmouth Shore and Southwick.

But many Wearsiders were dissatisfied with the Reform Act, for it only gave the vote to occupants of houses valued at £10 per annum or more, thereby excluding the vast majority of the working class. Hence 1839 witnessed the establishment of the Sunderland Charter Association; a local manifestation of a nationwide movement whose supporters (some of whom were middle class) subscribed to the 'People's Charter', a document which called, among other things, for universal male suffrage. Although some Chartists did not rule out resorting to violence, as Thomas Nossiter observes 'the tone of Wearside Chartism remained essentially non-violent.... If Sunderland was, as it was said, the headquarters of Durham Chartism, then it was a moral rather than a physical crusade in the county.'[2]

Sunderland's first MPs were both Liberals, namely Sir William Chaytor and Captain George Barrington, and in subsequent parliamentary elec-

1 *Ibid.*, p. 23.

2 T.J. Nossiter, *Influence, Opinion and Political Idioms in Reformed England: Case Studies from the North East 1832-1874*, 1975, p.155.

tions the winning candidates were usually Liberals as well. However, factionalism between different strands of liberalism—the Whigs and Radicals—meant that the Liberals were not as dominant as they could have been for on some occasions Whigs voted for Tory candidates.

Sunderland's most well-known Tory MP, George Hudson, was elected in the summer of 1845. The election excited interest well beyond the confines of Wearside and journalists came to Sunderland from the capital and elsewhere. Hudson, who had built up an impressive railway empire, was keen to enter the Commons so that he could argue his corner when a number of important railway bills came before the House.

He received an enthusiastic welcome on Wearside, especially as he promised to fulfill a desire of many of Sunderland's inhabitants, namely the construction of a south dock. As Michael Turner comments, Hudson 'had the resources and connections to carry the project forward. In persuading him to contest the by-election ... Sunderland's Conservatives knew they had done well for themselves.'[1] Not surprisingly, Hudson topped the poll on 14 August by gaining 627 votes, 129 more than his Radical opponent.

Suffrage was duly increased by the Parliamentary Reform Act of 1867. The number of registered electors in the constituency rose from 3,468 in 1866 to 11,364 and the winning candidates in the General Election of 1868 were both Radicals, Edward Temperley Gourley and John Candlish—the latter retained his seat, having been elected two years earlier at a by-election.

In subsequent contests during the period under discussion victorious candidates were always Liberals, as was true for example of Samuel Storey who had been born near Durham City in 1841 and settled at Monkwearmouth in 1864. He was elected to parliament in 1881.

Before becoming an MP, Storey had been a prominent local councillor—as noted above, as a result of the Municipal Corporations Act of 1835 Sunderland had gained a municipal council. The corporation's boundary embraced the bulk of the parliamentary borough but excluded Southwick. Initially, the municipal borough contained seven

---

1 M.J.Turner, 'Reform Politics and the Sunderland By-Election of 1845', *Northern History vol. XXXVIII, no.1, March 2001, p. 95.*

wards, each represented by six councillors and two aldermen, but under the Sunderland Extension and Improvement Act of 1867 two new wards were created, each represented by three councillors and an alderman.

Storey became a member of the town council in 1869 and emerged as the leading Radical councillor in the 1870s. He was elected mayor in 1876 (three years after he had co-founded the *Sunderland Echo*) and held the mayoralty for two other terms before entering parliament.

Among other things, the corporation was responsible for the establishment of the Sunderland Water Company in 1846—which began improving the quality of the town's water supply—and the formation of the Sunderland Gas Company in the same year. During the 1850s, moreover, the corporation implemented various measures to improve conditions in the town. These included the construction of public baths and wash houses, and the opening of the People's Park in 1857—now part of Mowbray Park. Furthermore, a large-scale sewerage system, comprising over 55 miles of drains, was installed in the second half of the 1850s and early 1860s.

Docks & Railways

This period witnessed the transformation of the port thanks to the construction of docks. The first of these, the North Dock, opened on the land of Sir Hedworth Williamson at Monkwearmouth Shore on 1 November 1837 and the first shipment of coal from the facility occurred in August 1839. The dock, however, was merely 9 acres in extent and only a modest level of activity took place.

Less than a decade later, in 1846, work began on a much larger dock on the south side of the river. Consequently, amid great pageantry on Thursday 20 June 1850 one of Sunderland's MPs, George Hudson, the 'Railway King', performed the opening ceremony. Of the event, which drew approximately 50,000 spectators, we read:

> At an early hour the feeling of the whole town was manifested by such crowded streets—crowded in every district, by dense assemblages of well-dressed and well-conducted persons—as we have never before witnessed.... The bells of the different churches rang out accordant peals, guns were fired at intervals, and the High Street (now one of the longest and best in old England, we

> beg to observe,) presented the most splendid and imposing aspect imaginable, the pavements, windows, parapets, and roofs of every building being densely crowded with anxious and impatient spectators.[1]

Shipments of coal from the 47-acre dock began the following month and, as had been anticipated, the new facilities provided a much-needed stimulus to the town's economy.

During the period under review, the local railway network, which had started to develop in the early decades of the century, expanded. The early lines carried coal to staithes lining the river bank just upstream of Wearmouth Bridge, a crossing that had opened in 1796. On the other hand, the Durham and Sunderland Railway, which began operating in 1836, likewise carried freight but it was also the first line in the history of Sunderland to carry passengers as well—passengers boarded or alighted at a station built on the Town Moor in the East End whereas coal was carried onward to staithes built on Low Quay. The line opened in stages. Initially, coal was carried to Sunderland from Hetton and Haswell whereas the early passenger service operated over a much shorter distance, namely between Sunderland and Ryhope. By 1839, however, the line had been extended to the outskirts of Durham City. Furthermore, owing to the undulating nature of the terrain over which the Durham and Sunderland operated, fixed engines hauled trains on this line, a state of affairs that lasted until 1855 when locomotives finally began to be used.

Other railways included the Brandling Junction Railway of 1839, whose southern terminus was at Monkwearmouth; and the Seaham and Sunderland Railway. The latter opened in 1854 to carry coal for shipment from the Wear—the harbour at Seaham was too small to cope with the enormous increase in the amount of coal needing to be exported—and a passenger service started the following year.

Local railway developments culminated with the opening of Sunderland Central Station in 1879 and the spanning of the Wear in the same year by a bridge to connect the railway networks on either side of the river.

1 *Sunderland Herald*, 21 June 1850, p. 5.

Monkwearmouth Railway Station

Sunderland Railway Bridge

Shipbuilding & Other Industries

In the 1850s it was observed that 'For all practical purposes, Sunderland is as new as an Australian or Yankee settlement.... We like the fresh-coloured vigour that characterises everything in Sunderland. There is no dreamy... indolence about the place.... They like their politics but they relish cash more.'[1]

The spirit of enterprise was certainly evident in the shipbuilding industry, a central facet of the local economy. Numerous yards existed in Sunderland and elsewhere on Wearside, and output reached a peak in 1840 when well over 64,000 tons were built. Sadly, fortunes then plummeted and many shipyards went under, so much so that in 1843 there were 31 on the Wear, less than half the pre-slump figure. Better times returned, though, in 1845 and five years later—when Sunderland's output surpassed New York's—the *Sunderland Herald* proudly declared that the town was 'the greatest shipbuilding port in the world.'[2]

The Wear's first iron ship, the *Loftus*, was built by George Clark and John Barkes and launched in 1852. Nevertheless, timber vessels continued to be built in large numbers thereafter and iron-built ships only formed the bulk of local output in the 1870s.

Sunderland's most well-known shipbuilder during this period was William Pile, who was born at Southwick in 1823 and was fascinated by ships from his youth. In 1848 he took over part of his father's yard at Monkwearmouth Shore and gained control of the rest of the yard in 1853. Pile was a consummate ship designer and his yard became the leading one on the Wear, employing two or three thousand workers. His most famous vessel, the *City of Adelaide* was launched in 1864—nine years before his death—and was of composite construction. In other words, it had an iron frame and a wooden hull, as was true of some other ships built on the Wear during these years.

Monkwearmouth Colliery was another major source of employment. The major task of sinking the pit through magnesian limestone lying

---

1 Anon., *Sketches of Public Men of the North*,1855, p. 56.

2 Quoted in J.F. Clarke, *Building Ships in the North East : A Labour of Love, vol, 1, c1640-1914*, 1997, p. 93. Over 51,000 tons were built on the Wear in 1850, albeit less than the total for 1840.

beneath Sunderland began in 1826 and the driving force behind the scheme was a local landowner, Richard Pemberton of Barnes—hence in its early years the mine was sometimes referred to as Pemberton Main. The first satisfactory seam, over 1,500ft below ground, was reached in the autumn of 1834 and production started the following year.

In the spring of 1841 John Roby Leifchild visited the mine to collect evidence for a Royal Commission Report on child labour. He was shocked to discover just how young some of the workforce was at Monkwearmouth and other pits he inspected in the region, for he encountered children as young as six. The management stated that working down the pit did not have a harmful effect on the youngsters but Leifchild's report cites evidence to the contrary. For instance, of a 12-year-old named John Bell, who worked as a driver, it records that he 'brings up his victuals from his stomach, perhaps three or four times in a fortnight ... His father says the pit does not agree with him.'[1] Although the ensuing Coal Mines Act of 1842 made it illegal for children under 10 to work underground, a couple of 9-year-olds were doing so at Monkwearmouth in 1851.

Sunderland's staple export was coal from Monkwearmouth and pits further afield. Other material exported included items manufactured by local potteries and glassworks. The largest pottery, Scott's, dated from 1788 and was located at Southwick. It was thus within the parliamentary borough of Sunderland but just outside the municipal boundary. The foremost glassworks, on the other hand—the Wear Glassworks—was founded at Deptford in 1836 by a young man of Scottish birth named James Hartley and because of his able and innovative leadership the business became one of the leading glass factories in the country. Indeed, in the 1860s the workforce numbered around 700.

Architecture

A number of fine buildings were erected in Sunderland between 1831 and 1881, and this is certainly true of Monkwearmouth Railway Station on North Bridge Street. This elegant Classical building, which opened in the summer of 1848, was designed by Thomas Moore (a blacksmith's

1 J.R. Leifchild, *Children's Employment Commission Report*, 1842, p. 644.

son born in Sunderland in 1794) and undoubtedly enhances the townscape.

Moore was little known beyond the confines of his hometown whereas Ignatius Bonomi, who designed Sunderland's first post-Reformation Catholic Church, St Mary's in Bridge Street, was far more prominent. He was born in London in 1787 and established a practice in Durham City in around 1809. For the exterior of St Mary's, which opened on Tuesday, 15 September 1835, Bonomi copied a style of medieval Gothic architecture termed Early English, one of whose motifs is the lancet window, and the façade of St Mary's is likewise dominated by generously-proportioned lancets.

St Mary's Church

St Mary's was not Sunderland's first Gothic Revival building—that honour belonged to Philip Wyatt's St Thomas' Church, erected in the heart of the town in 1829 and, regrettably, destroyed in an air raid in the Second World War.

Sunderland's most notable essay in the Gothic Revival idiom is however Christ Church in Ashbrooke, designed by James Murray of Coventry and completed in 1865. Of Christ Church, whose most eye-catching feature is a tower crowned by a lofty broach spire, it has been aptly observed that it 'was the first fully achieved Gothic Revival church in Sunderland.'[1]

On the other hand, banks favoured building in the Classical style. A case in point was the National Provincial Bank (now occupied by Morton's solicitors) in High Street West. The handsome premises opened

1 M. Johnson & G. Potts, *The Architecture of Sunderland, 1700-1914*, 2013, p. 63.

in 1878 and were designed by one of the foremost architects in his field, John Gibson.

Another architect who left his mark on Sunderland was Frank Caws, who was born on the Isle of Wight and settled on Wearside in 1867. Here, in 1870 at the age of 24, he began his own practice in Fawcett Street. Among other things, he designed the Elephant Tea House on the corner of Fawcett Street and High Street West, a 'Hindoo Gothic' building (his own expression) completed in 1877 and reminiscent of Indian architecture. Of Caws it has been aptly said: 'As an architect he combined sound knowledge of structure and engineering with an almost fanciful desire to be artistic and innovative and so produced some of the most distinctive and interesting buildings in Sunderland.'[1]

Religion & Education

Many of Sunderland's residents were religious, as was true for example of the glassmaker and politician James Hartley, who was raised a Methodist but joined the Church of England in 1853. Shortly before he did so a nationwide census was conducted in March 1851 to see how many people attended church or chapel, and Geoffrey Milburn comments:

> Organised religion was strong in Sunderland.... At the very minimum the total individual worshippers numbered over a quarter of the population, and the actual proportion was probably about one third.... Nonconformity, notably Methodism, was a dominant force in the religious and social life of the town, especially in the newly developing areas of Monkwearmouth and Bishopwearmouth.[2]

Owing to population growth and the physical expansion of the town, many new churches and chapels were built. One such, of course, was Christ Church, erected in the 1860s. Initially, Christ Church was a daughter of St Michael's (now Sunderland Minster) the spiritual heart of the vast parish of Bishopwearmouth. But the process of truncating the parish was well underway. For example, in 1844 two new parishes, St Thomas, Bishopwearmouth, and St Andrew's, Deptford, had been created. In the case of Christ Church, it remained a daughter of

1 G. Potts, 'Frank Caws, Sunderland Architect', *Sunderland's History* 10, 2003, p. 15.

2 G.E. Milburn, 'Religion in Sunderland in the mid 19th century' *Sunderland Polytechnic, Department of Geography and History Occasional paper No. 3*, 1983, p. 43.

Christ Church

St Michael's until 1875 when it too became a parish church. In the same year, Sunderland parish (formed from Bishopwearmouth in 1719) was reduced in size when St John's, an 18th-century Georgian chapel, was elevated to parish status.

Members of the clergy and different religious bodies founded some of the town's schools. In the mid 1830s, for instance, the Catholics set up a school just behind the recently built St Mary's Church on Bridge Street; while in 1849 the Presbyterians opened a school on Villiers Street that provided a fine education for as Milburn comments, the school 'soon acquired the title of "Academy", and offered a classical and commercial education for some 300 boys and girls which was considerably more advanced than could be had in the normal public elementary school.'[1]

As a result of an Act of Parliament passed in 1870, a school board was elected in Sunderland. The board's primary aim was to increase the number of elementary schools in the town and the first board school duly opened on James Williams Street in 1874. Elementary education was not compulsory at this date, a state of affairs that changed in 1880.

Recreation

Places of entertainment included the Theatre Royal in Drury Lane, an 18th-century venue that had been rebuilt in the late 1820s. According to George Patterson, 'by the 1840s the theatre was open six nights a week [although] the season remained restricted to the period February to April.' He continues:

> The stamina of the actors is astonishing.... Altogether there are 21 surviving bills for February and March 1845 and the only repeated performance is on Thursday 27 February.... So in 24 days the company performed at least 50 plays [and]... it is not surprising that critics at the time complained of under-rehearsed, incompetent performances.[2]

A rival concern, the Lyceum, opened on Lambton Street in 1852 and performers included Charles Dickens who came to Sunderland to perform in three plays at the newly opened venue on Saturday, 28 August, a point noted in the press:

> We can confidently say that never has there been gathered together in Sunderland an audience so numerous, distinguished,

1 G.E. Milburn, 'Education and Learning 1780-1914', in G.E. Milburn and S.T. Miller (eds.), *Sunderland – River, Town & People: A History from the 1780's to the Present Day*, 1988, p.143.

2 G. Patterson, *Sunderland's First Theatre & Music Hall*, 2009, p. 13.

> and enthusiastic, as that which greeted Mr Dickens and his friends, while the admirable arrangements and proportions of the room, the exquisite decorations of the stage and properties, and the brilliancy of the dresses, gave to the occasion an importance which will make it long remembered in the town.'[1]

Dickens returned to Wearside in 1858 and gave readings from his 'A Christmas Carol.' He did so at the Theatre Royal on Bedford Street, a venue that opened in late 1855 to replace the theatre on Drury Lane. Like the Lyceum, the new Theatre Royal was located close to the fashionable part of town.

Furthermore, from the mid 1850s music halls existed in the East End and were patronised by working class audiences. In fact in 1863 the old Theatre Royal, mostly closed since 1855, came to life again as the Wear Music Hall. It proved a success and was rebuilt on the same site in 1871 to provide larger and more comfortable premises.

Sports included cricket, which was well established when the period under discussion began, and in 1850 two clubs merged to form Sunderland Cricket Club based in Hendon. In 1876, though, having already moved once in the interim, the club settled beside Chester Road. The club shared the premises with Sunderland Rugby Football Club, founded in 1873. Moreover, in the closing year of the decade a local schoolmaster was responsible for founding a football team manned by fellow members of the teaching profession. In 1881 membership was opened up to non-teachers and the name was changed to Sunderland Association Football Club, an institution which of course still survives and has become a central facet of Sunderland's identity.

I have dealt with this theme more fully in 'As new as an Australian or Yankee Settlement—Sunderland in the Years 1831-1881', published by the Architectural and Archaeological Society of Durham & Northumberland in the *Durham Archaeological journal*, volume 19, 2014, pp 133-161.

---

1 *Sunderland Herald*, 3 September 1852, p. 5.

BENJAMIN SWINHOE & THE *EARL OF DUMFRIES*

On the afternoon of Thursday, 30 June 1904, a tugboat named the *Earl of Dumfries* towed a Norwegian schooner into the South Dock of Sunderland's harbour. After mooring the sailing vessel, at around 4.00pm the tugboat steamed out of the dock via the south outlet (which gave direct access to the sea) and thus commenced yet another journey in search of a ship to bring into the port.

The captain of the *Earl of Dumfries* was Benjamin Swinhoe, and of his occupation Robert Moon has commented: 'The bringing of both sailing and steam-ships into the docks was ... a highly skilled operation ... [that] required expert towing from the tugs. The tug captain was an underrated and yet highly skilled master of his profession.'[1]

Benjamin Swinhoe was born on 8 May 1851 and was baptised in Holy Trinity Church, Sunderland, on the 25th. He came from a seafaring family and his parents, Benjamin and Eleanor (née Watson), born in Sunderland in 1823 and 1825 respectively, were then resident at 23 Silver Street. This once fashionable road, whose status had declined by the mid 19th century, dated from the early 18th century, was roughly aligned north to south, and lay deep in Sunderland's East End. Benjamin was the couple's third child and the census states that his father was a pilot. However, his name does not appear in the Sunderland Pilotage Commission Register of Pilots—much to the chagrin of genuine pilots, they faced competition from unlicensed individuals who piloted vessels in and out of the river.

In 1851 Sunderland's population numbered approximately 64,000, of whom around 19,000 lived in the East End, that is, the parish of Sunderland. The parish dated from 1719 and had previously been part of the much larger parish of Bishopwearmouth.

The main source of employment in Sunderland was seafaring. Many other residents of the town derived their livelihoods from shipbuilding

---

1 R. Moon, *The Sundered- Land: the Story of a Seaport and its Township*, 2008, p. 104.

and related industries (making ropes and sails for instance) and in the year of Swinhoe's birth there were approximately 2,000 shipwrights.

By 1861 the Swinhoes were living at 9 Bank Street in the East End and Benjamin's father was employed as a steamboat captain, likely the master of a tugboat. Bank Street lay little more than a stone's throw to the northeast of Silver Street but, unlike it, was located just to the north of the neighbourhood's main thoroughfare, High Street East. Bank Street was aligned roughly parallel to the River Wear and lay on ground that sloped down towards the quayside—the street survived until the 1930s when it was among property demolished to make way for the construction of the Corporation Quay.

In 1861 many children received little or no schooling—elementary education only became compulsory in 1880—but Benjamin was more fortunate. The census notes that he was a 'scholar.' So, too, were his three sisters, whose ages ranged from 4 to 12.

They may well have been pupils of the Gray School (it was referred to at the time as the 'Gray Schools' because there were separate departments for boys and girls) named in memory of the philanthropic and highly conscientious clergyman Robert Gray, Rector of Sunderland in the years 1819-38. The school was founded for boys in 1808 and was initially located near Holy Trinity Church. In 1823, however, by which time girls had also been admitted, it moved northeast to Vine Street,

The only known photograph of the *Earl of Dumfries*

where it remained until 1857. In the latter year, it relocated to purpose-built premises erected on land hitherto part of Sunderland's shrinking Town Moor. The new site was about a minute's walk to the east of Holy Trinity: the premises were on the east side of Quadrant Street, which ran between the school and the Trafalgar Square almshouses closer to the parish church.

The year 1863 witnessed the death of Benjamin's mother Eleanor, whose name was sometimes given as 'Ellen'. When she went to her grave, aged 38, Ben was perhaps about to start life as a mariner for during this era it was commonplace for boys of around 12 or 13 to go to sea. Such a life, fraught with hardship, excitement and danger, could take them to far-flung destinations, as was true for example of the Wearsider John Todd (1840-99) who went to sea at the age of 15 and whose first voyage was to Burma. More typical, were journeys along England's east coast, carrying cargoes, especially coal—the Wear's staple export—to London and elsewhere.

The census of 1871 shows that Benjamin's father had remarried. Once again, though, the family was still resident in the East End for their address was 1 Stone Yard, just to the north of Bank Street. The house was one of several dwellings located along a secluded and indirect passageway that lead down to the quayside. However, the future master of the *Earl of Dumfries* does not appear on the census and was presumably at sea.

A few years later, when in his mid 20s, Benjamin married. He did so at St Peter's Church, Monkwearmouth, on 13 November 1875 and his young bride was Mary Isabella Thompson, the daughter of a shipwright named Richard. The marriage certificate states that the couple's address was 27 Zetland Street, Monkwearmouth, and also notes that Benjamin's father was still a steamboat captain.

Swinhoe's wife had been baptised at Sunderland parish church, Holy Trinity, on 6 March 1857. Moreover, in 1871 her home had been located in Bank Street. A narrow archway on the north side of Bank Street led to a flight of wooden stairs. These descended to the Stone Yard where of course the Swinhoes were resident at the time of the 1871 census. It is thus possible that Benjamin and Mary became acquainted while living in the East End.

St. Peter's church

Within a few months of marrying, the newly-weds had their first child, Benjamin, who came into the world at 27 Low Street in the East End on 3 February 1876. Sadly, though, his life was brief for he died in December 1877.

By then, Mary had recently given birth to another son. Furthermore, the subsequent census of 1881 records two more children. It also mentions that the Swinhoes were at 8 Bank Street; an address they were sharing with Robert Bailey, a 58-year-old blacksmith and his wife. Later that year, the Swinhoe family was enlarged by the birth of another son, the second child to be named Benjamin.

In his leisure moments, Swinhoe—now a master mariner—probably enjoyed visiting public houses. These were numerous in the East End and several lay close to his residence, as was true for example of the *Turk's Head* at 116 High Street East. On other occasions, Benjamin may have enjoyed performances at the Wear Music Hall in the East End's Drury Lane, where 'variety' artistes had proved very popular since the lively venue had opened in 1863. Presumably, family outings included visits to the People's Park (opened in 1857) and the adjoining Extension Park (opened 1866) both of which have since become Mowbray Park. They also probably visited Sunderland Museum and Library, which occupied imposing purpose-built premises on Borough Road after relocating from Fawcett Street in 1879. Doubtless, too, the family sometimes crossed the Wear by ferry to visit the seafront at Roker, an area whose attraction had been enhanced by the opening of Roker Park in 1880.

Benjamin likely maintained contact with his father and by 1881 the latter, who was still employed as a steamboat captain, was no longer in the East End. He had moved the short distance southward to 18 Lawrence Street, Hendon, his home since at least 1878. He was dwelling there with his Scottish-born third wife, together with a 22-year-old son James Swinhoe (a mercantile insurance clerk) and stepchildren. Also present, and employed as the family's general servant, was 22-year-old Emma Hall from London.[1] Another change of address however ensued, for when Benjamin senior died on 17 September 1884 he was living at 123 Herrington Street in Bishopwearmouth, Sunderland.

Less than two years after the death of his father, the future master of the *Earl of Dumfries* experienced another bereavement. By this time he and his family were resident in North Moor Street (a continuation of High Street East) which terminated near the entrance of the South Dock. The death occurred following an incident at around 7.30pm on 8 June 1886. Of the event, we read:

> Last evening an accident attended with fatal consequences occurred to a boy named Benjamin Swinhoe on the South Dock near to the Coast Guard houses. It appears that the deceased [who had recently celebrated his fifth birthday]...was playing with other boys about some waggons which were standing on an incline near to the place indicated. Swinhoe...was underneath one of the waggons which started to run and passed over both his thighs, nearly severing them from the body. He was taken to the Infirmary, but it was at once seen that his life could not be saved and he died about nine o'clock.[2]

---

1 Interestingly, four brothers resident in 17 Lawrence Street had been born in Australia, whereas their widower father, 50-year-old James Hay (a bookkeeper) had been born in Sunderland, as was true of his unmarried sister who was likewise living at the same address.

2 *Sunderland Echo*, Wednesday, 9 June 1886, p. 3.

Mary Isabella Swinhoe (left)

Benjamin Swinhoe duly identified his son's body. According to an inquest held at the Infirmary on the following Friday, the accident had been caused when one of the boys removed a chock holding the waggons in place. Other youngsters had then pushed the waggons in order to have a ride.

At this date, Benjamin was the captain of a steam tug named the *Echo.* Although some vessels were still powered by sail—the Wear's last sailing ship would be built in 1893—tugs had been the first craft on the Wear to use steam propulsion; a state of affairs that dated from the 1820s. Swinhoe was fortunate to have employment. The mid 1880s was a dire period for many Wearsiders, largely as a result of a depression that had affected the town's shipyards.

The name 'Benjamin' evidently mattered to Swinhoe, for in late 1890 when Mary gave birth to another son he was likewise given the name. The newcomer was four months old at the time of the following census, which notes that his father was a master mariner and that the family was living at 18 Commissioners' Quay, the easternmost on the river and close to the entrance of the South Dock. They shared the property with seven other people, members of two families.

From his home, Benjamin could look across the river at one of Sunderland's leading shipyards, J.L. Thompson's, which was located at North Sands, Monkwearmouth. Presumably, at times he reflected on the enormous changes that had occurred on the Wear during his own lifetime. When he was born in 1851, ships built on Wearside were all constructed of wood. Although February of the following year had witnessed the launch of the Wear's first iron vessel it was not until the 1870s that iron construction had become dominant. Its ascendancy proved short-lived, though, for in the 1880s steel construction had become the norm.

On 6 December 1897 Benjamin's twelfth and final child was born at 7 Ettrick Quay which, as its name indicates, overlooked the river and was in fact close to Bank Street. The latest addition to the family was christened Hannah Isabella Elliott Swinhoe and baptised at Holy Trinity Church. In contrast, almost all of Benjamin's other children had been baptised at St John's Church which lay a few minutes' walk to the east of Holy Trinity and had been built as a chapel of ease in the 1760s. St John's had become a parish church in its own right in 1875.

Conditions in the East End were poor for most of the 19th century and had reportedly worsened in recent decades, largely as a result of an influx of hapless newcomers attracted by low rents on offer. The area was characterised by poverty and heavy drinking. Gambling and prostitution were likewise more prevalent than was true of Sunderland as a whole.

In 1896 a report on St John's Parish, which covered most of the East End, noted: 'From the irregular labourer to the man whose stock in trade is a tin whistle there are gradations of employment unheard of in other sections of society. They live, or rather drag out, a hand-to-mouth existence... and are in that chronic state of poverty which makes a dole always acceptable.'[1] The report also says that low church attendance at St John's was partly attributable to the fact that some parishioners were too ashamed of the state of their clothing to attend services.

Why Benjamin Swinhoe continued to reside in the East End is unclear. Perhaps he chose to remain in order to be close to his place of employment. What is certain is that as a tugboat captain he belonged to the upper tier of East End society and enjoyed a better income than many Eastenders.

By 1901 the Swinhoes were living at 7 Low Quay—a short distance

1 *The East End of Sunderland. St John's Parish: its work and its limitations,*1896, pp. 14-15.

downriver of Ettrick's Quay. Benjamin was now the captain of a wooden paddle tug, the *Earl of Glamorgan*, which had been built at North Shields and had been completed in 1869. He and his wife shared the address with five of their daughters and their two sons. One of the daughters was employed as a domestic housemaid and the other as a tobacconist's assistant.

In subsequent years Benjamin continued to captain tugboats and in late 1902 or shortly thereafter he became the master of the *Earl of Dumfries*, an iron tug built at Cardiff in 1882 with a net tonnage of 9.61 tons and 50hp engines. The vessel was over 87ft long, exceeded 17ft in width, and was more than 9ft in depth. Her owners included Thomas Hutchinson of Monkwearmouth, who possessed 36 shares in the tugboat in 1904. Repairs were undertaken by Messrs William Hepple and Co. of South Shields and by the local firm of Messrs Lindsay, Caverhill and Co. On 29 September 1903 the tug had passed an annual survey, at which time the hull, boilers and machinery were deemed to be in good condition. Moreover there was suitable lifesaving equipment.

The paddle tug *Earl of Glamorgan*

As noted above, the *Earl of Dumfries* left the south outlet of Sunderland harbour late on the afternoon of 30 June 1904. Having done so, she headed southeast in the hope of finding a ship to bring into the port. En route the tug passed within 50 yards or so of a fishing smack named *Ethereal* whose skipper, Thomas Davison of Sunderland, was making for crab pots just beyond Seaham Harbour. Davison caught sight of Benjamin Swinhoe at the helm and subsequently, at around 5.10pm—by which time the *Earl of Dumfries* was about half a mile to the west of the *Ethereal*—he heard a deafening sound and saw that fragments of the tug had been blasted into the air amid a cloud of steam. He also heard two explosions.[1] The *Ethereal* thus headed towards the site of the stricken craft which, owing to the force of the explosion, was now facing in the opposite direction to the one in which it had been heading. Upon arriving about 15 minutes after the disaster—a contrary wind hindered progress—they merely found an oil drum, a mat and oil bottle as well as ashes strewn on the surface.

Further details are provided by a local newspaper:

> Shortly before five o'clock several persons at the docks observed a tug making for a schooner to the south. When about three miles east of Seaham Harbour a tremendous volume of steam obscured the tug, the boiler, it is supposed, having burst, as in a few seconds all trace of the vessel had disappeared.
>
> The schooner which the tug had apparently been making for was about a mile to the south of the tug when the explosion occurred, and passed over the spot where the steam tug went down. She was not observed from the shore to have hauled to and it is supposed that no trace of the crew was to be seen when she reached the spot.[2]

Benjamin Swinhoe was the only one of the fatalities who lived in the East End. He left a widow and a family of nine, three of whom were grown up. The engineer, John Wake and the other crew members Thomas Swallow, the senior fireman, and Richard Hutchinson the junior

1 The time of the incident is uncertain. Some witnesses said that the explosion happened at around 4.50pm. On the other hand, Charles Cook, a witness at the subsequent Board of Inquiry (he was a tugboat master) stated that from the pilots' lookout house near Hendon Dock he had seen the *Earl of Dumfries* as it left the south outlet at around 4.20, and that he also saw the tug shortly after 5.00 o'clock.

2 *Sunderland Echo*, Friday 1 July 1904, p. 6.

fireman, all lived in Monkwearmouth. Hutchinson was the youngest of the men and the only one who was single. He was a relative of the tugboat's registered owner, Thomas Hutchinson.

Furthermore, we read:

> it is feared that the death toll will increase to five. In addition to the four men constituting the crew of the tug, there was on board the vessel during the afternoon Robert Wright, aged about forty years. This man, also from Monkwearmouth, has no fixed place of abode and for years had made his home on tugs. He found the unfortunate crew of the Earl of Dumfries kind to him, being supplied by them with food, and he was continually out in the tug. In fact he was like one of the crew.[1]

At the subsequent Board of Inquiry a witness named James Ailley, a boatman, said that Wright was about 45 and that he had seen him aboard the *Earl of Dumfries* when she put to sea for the last time.

Several days later, on the evening of Monday 4 July a large number of people, including several members of Sunderland Corporation, attended a meeting of the Steamboatmen's Society held at the Seamen's Mission (today's Exchange Building) in the East End. The aim was 'to devise some means of alleviating the suffering and distress brought upon several families through the sad disaster to the steam tug Earl of Dumfries.'[2]

The event was presided over by a local councillor, Ralph Annison, who said that he 'would like to impress upon everyone who intended to take some active part in connection with the effort that there was nothing that cooled so soon as sympathy and consequently there was great need for immediate action.'[3]

During the proceedings a letter from Handley Moule, the Bishop of Durham, was read out expressing his sadness at the tugboat's loss and his feelings of sympathy for the bereaved. The correspondence

---

1 *Ibid.*, p. 6.

2 *Seaham Weekly News*, Friday 8 July 1904, p. 8.

3 *Sunderland Echo*, Tuesday 5 July 1904, p. 3. Annison, incidentally, had played a key role in events that had resulted in the construction of the memorial to Jack Crawford (1775-1831) in Mowbray Park.

had been sent to Douglas Samuel Boutflower, the Vicar of St Peter's, Monkwearmouth.

At the meeting a committee was appointed—some of the members were tugboat owners—and one of those chosen for this role, namely the Reverend Aubrey Leake of St John's Church, proposed holding a memorial service. Moreover, Councillor Edwin Shields (also chosen to serve on the committee) intimated that Charles Machin, the managing director of the Avenue Theatre in Bishopwearmouth, had promised that the venue could be used without payment to hold a benefit concert for the dependents of the dead crewmen.

The evening then concluded with a meeting of the committee, at which it was decided that its members should be allocated specific areas of the town in which to raise funds for the task at hand. Arrangements were also made to hold a memorial service on Sunday, 17 July.

On Monday 18 July, Councillor Annison once again presided when the committee held another meeting at the Seamen's Mission. He stated that £155 9s. 9d. had been raised so far and that subscriptions promised would result in a total of £500 or more. For his part, Councillor Shields said that it had been arranged that the East End Prize Band concert would take place on the Lower Promenade on Thursday 28 July and that collecting boxes would be sent around to receive donations for the fund.

On Monday the 25th the committee met again. Of the proceedings we read:

> The scheme which was organised by a number of Sunderland gentlemen a short while ago for the alleviation of the distress caused by the explosion of the tug boat Earl of Dumfries off Seaham Harbour ... was practically brought to a close on Monday night last at a public meeting in the Seamen's Institute, presided over by Coun. R.B. Annison. During the three weeks the fund had been in existence, a total sum of £573 18s 11d. had been collected, and there are still several collecting boxes and books to be got in. This money is to be divided in the following manner among the three families who suffered by the sad disaster. The captain's widow, Mrs Sweeney [Swinhoe], will receive a total sum of £166, to be extended over a period of three years; Mrs Wake, who has a family of eight, will receive a total sum of £270 in five years, and efforts will be made to get one of the boys into the Sunderland

> Orphan Asylum, and also to obtain the Hudson Charity; and Mrs Swallow, who is a dressmaker in somewhat better circumstances, will receive £88 in three years making a grand total of £524. If at the end of the periods mentioned all the money is not exhausted, the remainder will be handed over to the Sunderland Orphanage.[1]

The sums granted to the bereaved were far from negligible, a point illustrated by the fact that when Sunderland's first council housing, Harrison's Building, had opened in the East End the previous year the weekly rent for a three-room flat was 5s. 6d.

On Thursday, 28 July 1904, a Board of Trade Inquiry was held at the Education Offices in Sunderland to investigate the loss of the tugboat. The chairman was Captain J.W. Squance while lawyers present included James Storey, a solicitor acting for Thomas Hutchinson, the registered managing owner of the tug, and R.S. Middleton, a solicitor representing the relatives of Benjamin Swinhoe.

Thomas Hutchinson told the hearing, among other things, that Benjamin 'was a man of long experience among tugs. The engineer was also experienced, but he had no certificate. The crew as a whole were of good character—he had never had a better one.'[2] Moreover, he said that the master of the tugboat was authorised to have any repairs done that he deemed necessary.

Furthermore, Hutchinson's solicitor outlined expenditure on maintenance and repair work that had been undertaken to the *Earl of Dumfries* since 1895, and declared that there was abundant evidence to prove that she was in good and seaworthy condition.

For their part, William Thomas Hepple and John George Caverhill spoke about work their firms had carried out on the owners' behalf. For example, Caverhill told the court that from the beginning of January 1900 until 27 May 1904 his firm had undertaken 'sundry repairs' to the *Earl of Dumfries*.

---

1 *Seaham Weekly News*, Friday, 29 July 1904, p. 8. Incidentally, the Orphan Asylum dated from 1861 and was situated a short distance to the south of Holy Trinity Church; whereas the Hudson Charity was set up under the terms of the will of George Hudson (1800-84) a wealthy local shipowner and shipbuilder, and gave financial assistance to orphan boys and girls.

2 *Sunderland Echo*, July 28 1904, p. 3.

Thomas Denby, who had been the engineer on the tug until shortly before the disaster (he left the vessel on 4 June) told the inquiry that whilst he was engineer new spring valves were put into the boilers. To this, however, one of the nautical assessors, Mr Gray, replied that it was a serious matter to have done so without first ensuring that the boilers were capable of carrying a pressure of 30 lbs.

At the end of proceedings Captain Squance announced that judgement would be given at noon the following day.

Hence at the appointed hour on Friday, 29 July, he declared that when the *Earl of Dumfries* had put to sea for the last time she 'was in a good and seaworthy condition, but the boilers and their mountings were not in good working order.' No evidence, he continued, had been presented to the inquiry to prove that the boilers had ever been tested in the last five years to show that they could withstand a pressure exceeding 30 lbs, a pressure to which they had been subjected routinely. What is more, since 1901 'no exhaustive examination of the boilers had been made to test their condition.' Instead, evidence had been

> given to the effect that they were in good condition 'for their age,' and in better order than many boats of this class which were passed for sea. The Court had been very much impressed by these statements, and thought that in the interests of the crews and the public at large it was high time the really appalling state of affairs which exists among this class of vessels was brought to the notice of the Board of Trade.'[1]

Of Thomas Hutchinson, it was judged that he had evidently carried out repairs he thought to be necessary. However, in view of the loss of the tugboat it would have been better if he had received expert guidance on the matter. The court, however, decided not to attach any blame to him over the tragedy for he had acted in accord with the 'general practice in vogue on this class of vessel.'[2]

Sadly, no photograph of Benjamin Swinhoe apparently exists. However, a letter written by his youngest son and namesake on 30 July 1975[3] states that he 'wore gold wire earrings' and was 'a typical "Old

1 *Sunderland Echo*, 29 July 1904, p. 6.

2 *Ibid.*

3 The letter was penned in Vancouver, Canada, and sent to his nephew David John Dodds, a resident of Sunderland.

Salt."' Furthermore, the son recalled that he had accompanied his father to a becalmed sailing ship named the *Alderson,* which Benjamin proceeded to tow further out to sea so that the vessel caught a southward wind. Moreover, the letter continues:

> I've seen father tow two ships in together, leave one outside the harbour, and as soon as the other one got tied up at the buoys, dash out to bring in the other one from the Baltic loaded with pit props and ties for the Railways. Those were the days also when the big iron sailing ships used to bring in the grain from Australia to discharge at the granary at the South Dock. In my younger days it was a wonderful sight to see a full-rigged ship sailing by.

Benjamin Swinhoe's youngest son—also called Benjamin

Several years after the disaster, the census of 1911 recorded that Benjamin Swinhoe's widow, Mary, was living in a two-room residence in the Sheepfolds area of Sunderland and was accompanied by her youngest child, 13-year-old 'Bella.' Shortly, thereafter, for one reason or another Mary left her hometown and ended her days in South Shields in 1913. Doubtless from time to time she had cast her mind back to the events of 30 June 1904 which had so dramatically ended the life of her husband and everyone else on board the ill-fated *Earl of Dumfries.*

I wish to thank Derek Haynes (a fellow great-grandson of Benjamin Swinhoe) for providing some of the information used in this chapter.

The First Decade of the Sunderland Antiquarian Society

As Queen Victoria's reign drew to a close a group of gentlemen met in the heart of Sunderland to discuss forming a society dedicated to exploring and recording the town's past.

Of events, we read:

> In response to a Circular issued by Mr. G.W. Bain, a meeting of gentlemen favourable to the formation of an Antiquarian Society was held in the Board Room of the Industrial and Provident Building Society, 42 Fawcett Street, Sunderland, on Tuesday, 21st November, 1899.

After a statement by Mr. Bain it was formally resolved to form such a Society, to be called 'The Sunderland Antiquarian Society.'[1]

Subsequently, on Tuesday, 5 December, several statutes were devised and adopted. For one thing, membership would not be open to everyone. Names of prospective members were to be 'submitted to the Council of the Society' and could be rejected. If, however, the name was accepted by the council it would then be placed before a general meeting where the individual could 'be elected by a simple majority.'

The society's 'inaugural meeting' was held in the above-mentioned boardroom on Thursday, 1 February 1900—the date is wrongly given as Tuesday, 1 February, in the first volume of the society's journal—and Thomas Randell was elected president. Born in Wiltshire in 1848, Randell had attended four universities, including Trinity College, Dublin, where he had gained a doctorate in divinity. He was Rector of Sunderland, a post he had held since 1892.

Among other members of the society's first council were George Washington Bain and James Patterson. The former was an insurance broker who had been born in Ireland in 1855 and had settled in Sunderland in 1876. He became the society's first chairman. Patterson, on the other hand,

---

1 'First Annual Report', *Antiquities of Sunderland*, vol. 1, 1902, p. 39.

was born in Bishopwearmouth in 1846. He had married into the Hills family, which ran a bookshop founded in 1852, and helped to manage the business located in Fawcett Street.

Initially, the society's annual subscription was five shillings and the vast majority of the antiquaries were well-to-do. Their backgrounds, however, were certainly diverse. For instance, Henry Reginald Leighton, who lived at East Boldon, was the scion of Northumbrian gentry. On the other hand, Alderman William Burns, a Scot whose name also appears on membership lists from 1900 onward, was born into humble circumstances but had founded a successful grocery business in Hendon in around 1860. He served as Mayor of Sunderland from November 1895 to November 1897 and lived in Grange Crescent, Ashbrooke, an affluent neighbourhood where a high proportion of his fellow antiquaries likewise resided.

At a meeting held at 42 Fawcett Street on Tuesday, 6 March 1900, one of the society's founding fathers, John Robinson—described as a 'gentleman' in a local directory—read a lucid and generally well informed paper entitled 'Sunderland Church and Parish.' Holy Trinity, the subject of the article, was consecrated on 5 September 1719 and was one of the first brick churches in County Durham. Of it, Robinson observed:

> There is nothing attractive about the architecture of The Holy Trinity Church, or Sunderland Church as it is more frequently called and it lacks the warm colouring which age gives to so many of our English Churches. But once inside the sacred building, it has quite an attractive appearance and has its own peculiar beauties.[1]

The first volume of the society's journal, *Antiquities of Sunderland*, notes that one intention of the founders was to 'organise excursions to places of antiquarian interest, especially those near Sunderland, so as to make pleasure contribute in some degree to an intelligent knowledge of the antiquities and historical associations of the district, and, indirectly, of other localities also.'[2]

Excursions took place at least once a year during the period dealt with by this article, and the first trip in the society's history occurred on Saturday, 7 July 1900, when members travelled to Durham by train from Sun-

1 *Antiq. Sund.*, vol. I, p. 5.

2 *Ibid.*, p. xv.

derland Central Station. They were welcomed at the cathedral by Canon William Greenwell who gave the group a conducted tour of the magnificent church. According to the *Sunderland Echo*, Greenwell 'conducted them to the most interesting features in the building, explaining in detail the events leading up to the commencement and completion of the edifice.'[1] The paper also states that Greenwell conducted the visitors around Durham Castle but this is not mentioned in the society's minutes.

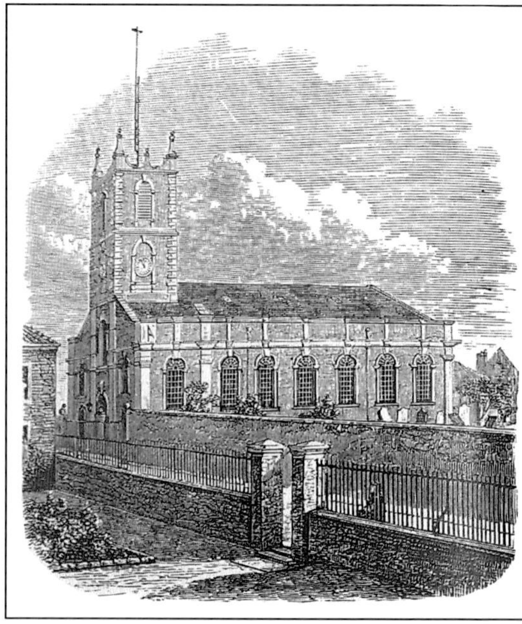

Holy Trinity Church

Shortly thereafter, on Tuesday 29 January 1901 the society's council decided that future meetings would be held in the Subscription Library, which had occupied substantial purpose-built premises in Fawcett Street since 1878.

The first volume of *Antiquities of Sunderland* was printed in 1902 by the local firm of S.A. Forster. The *Sunderland Herald* of Saturday, 6 September 1902, gave a favourable review but noted: 'It seems a pity that it should not have been offered for sale. The general public would gladly have seized the opportunity of purchasing this interesting and instructive account of the work of our local antiquaries... [presented] in such an eminently attractive form.'

The subsequent annual report for 1902, jointly penned by the

1 *Sunderland Echo*, 9 July 1900, p. 3. Whereas the first volume of the society's journal states that the excursion party numbered 26, the *Echo* says that the party was between 40 and 50 strong: perhaps the latter figure includes non-members of the society.

chairman James Patterson and the honorary secretary Benjamin Rowland Hill, chided the 101-strong membership. It states: 'Your Council... think it right to point out that good and interesting as the Papers have been, they were contributed by only a very few of the Members. The Council would urge all Members to take part in this primary work by contributing Notes and Papers on matters of local interest.'[1] Presumably, matters were exacerbated by the society's policy of only allowing material to be published in the journal after it had been read at meetings, an off-putting stance to would-be contributors of shy disposition.

In early 1904 Randell was succeeded as president by the Reverend John Thomas Middlemiss who was in his late forties and had been born in Morpeth. He had served as the popular pastor of the Presbyterian Church in North Bridge Street since 1886 and lived in Roker Park Road.

Of the society's excursions in 1904, we read:

> There were... held during the year two Out-door Meetings, viz., to Finchale Priory on the 9th July, when those present were favoured with remarkably fine weather, at which Meeting Mr. James Patterson read a paper on 'The origin and history of the ruin,' and to the Old Castle and Black Gate, Newcastle-on-Tyne, on the 24th September, both of which were largely attended by the members and their friends.[2]

Nonetheless, the year witnessed a fall in membership. Thomas Ray, the chairman, therefore stated in the annual report: 'There are at present 87 members of the Society, as against 109 last year. During the year 10 new members have been elected, and 22 members have resigned.'[3] In addition, there were nine institutional members including the Bodlein Library in Oxford.

In 1905 the society's patron since its formation, John George Lambton, the third Earl of Durham, became a member. Furthermore, on Tuesday 7 November of the same year the society enjoyed a visit from Count Mörner of Stockholm, who gave a talk and exhibited his collection of Napoleonic material. At this meeting there were a large number

---

1 *Antiq. Sund.*, vol. 3, 1904, p. 121.

2 *Antiq. Sund.*, vol. V, 1907 p. 71.

3 *Ibid.*, p. 70.

of visitors present, including many ladies. The presence of females was a novelty. Only the previous day, James Patterson had declared: 'Except at summer excursions, ladies are not admitted to the deliberations of the Society, but in view of the especially interesting features of this meeting, it has been decided on this occasion to invite lady friends of members.'[1]

George W. Bain became the society's third president early in 1906. The list of members for that year contains 77 names and shows that one of the newcomers was Sir William Theodore Doxford of Grindon Hall, who ran the largest shipyard on the Wear.

On Wednesday 22 August 1906, members of the society enjoyed an excursion to Holy Island. It was the most far-flung outing so far and included a hair-raising departure from the tidal island: 'After tea the party left the Island by brakes [horse-drawn vehicles] across the sand which proved a unique experience as the tide was up to the axles of the vehicles, thus creating some excitement. The party eventually arrived in Sunderland at 11 p.m., after having spent a most enjoyable day.'[2]

Minutes for a meeting held on Wednesday, 15 January 1908, record that Bain successfully proposed that James Patterson should be his successor as president: 'he spoke in a eulogistic manner of the many qualifications Mr. Patterson held for that post and the great interest and energy he had always displayed in the affairs of the society.'

Interestingly, just over a year later minutes of a meeting held on Tuesday 16 March 1909 record that 'the President before opening the proceedings expressed his great pleasure in welcoming Mrs C.H. Elliott the first lady member of the society.' Elliott (whose husband was also a member) lived at 5 Eden Place, Newcastle Road.

Subsequently, on Tuesday 13 October, a member of the society named James Porteous Cornett, who lived in South Hylton, read a paper on Wearside's paper industry; an industry which had begun in around 1826 when a paper mill opened in the industrial suburb of Deptford. Cornett had first hand experience of his subject for since 1883 he had been the manager of Ford Paper Mill, which commenced operating in the summer of 1838. Among other things, Cornett stated:

> The Ford and Hendon mills are now the only two mills existing

1 D. W. Smith, 'The Antiquarian Founding Fathers', *Sunderland's History* 11, 2005, p. 56.

2 *Antiq. Sund.*, vol. VII, 1908, p. 83.

> in Sunderland [Hendon Paper Works had opened in 1872], but it is interesting to know that there are still seven mills in the county of Durham probably turning out an aggregate of about 600 tons weekly of white paper principally... and... giving direct employment to over 1,000 workpeople.[1]

The tenth annual report was read in the smokeroom of Sunderland Subscription Library on Tuesday 8 February 1910 and 'showed that the society maintained its prosperous condition.' Moreover 'the council recorded the sense of loss the society felt at the departure of the Rev. Dr. Randell... who did much useful work on the formation of the society, and they congratulated him on his preferment to Ryton.'[2] It was also noted that the eighth volume of the journal had been published and that T. Coke Squance, a medical doctor born in Sunderland in around 1851, had been elected the society's president, thereby replacing Patterson. Squance had joined the society in 1905 and lived in Grange Crescent.

Shortly thereafter the *Sunderland Echo* of Friday, 8 April 1910, contained an illustration of the logo recently adopted by the society and designed on its behalf by a member, namely the local architect, John Hall, FRIBA. The society's badge features the entrance arch of St Peter's Church and contains a number of Anglo-Saxon motifs.

By now it was just over a decade since the Sunderland Antiquarian Society had been formed. Much had been achieved since the society's formation and a firm foundation had certainly been laid for future growth. Indeed, the society has never again been as dynamic or productive as it was in these exciting years.

I have dealt with this theme at greater length in 'Learned Papers & Excursions—the first decade of the Sunderland Antiquarian Society', *Durham County Local History Society Journal 79*, 2014, pp. 82-101.

---

1 J.P. Cornish, 'The Paper Mills of Sunderland', *Antiq. Sund.*, vol. 9, 1910, p. 164. The mill at Deptford had closed in 1902. For its part, Hendon Paper Works became the largest paper mill in the North East and employed over 400 people in the early 20th century.

2 *Sunderland Echo*, 9 Februrary 1910, p. 3.

Sunderland During World War Two

King George VI and Queen Elizabeth received an enthusiastic reception on Thursday 19 June 1941 when they visited Doxford's shipyard—the largest on the Wear. The royal couple 'walked slowly among groups of men sitting about the yard eating their lunch, and chatted with them about a hundred and one different things.'[1]

The visit acknowledged the important role Sunderland's shipbuilding industry was playing in the nation's fight for survival. Most of the vessels constructed on the Wear were merchant ships, and an indication of the town's contribution to wartime production can be gained from the fact that in the period from September 1939 to the end of 1944, around 27 per cent of the total output of merchant shipping from all British yards was produced in Sunderland, a considerable achievement.

Inevitably, the shipyards attracted the unwelcome attention of the Luftwaffe, for German aircraft repeatedly bombed Sunderland from the summer of 1940 onward, and in anticipation of this onslaught, several thousand Wearsiders were evacuated from the town in September 1939 shortly after the war had started. They bordered trains at Monkwearmouth, Millfield and Pallion on two successive days. Nevertheless, partly because many families found the idea of separation too painful, most of Sunderland's children remained at home. Under a heading entitled 'Evacuation Indifference', it was noted on Tuesday, 12 September: 'Instead of 6,000 mothers and young children taking train yesterday only 1,785 of those who had registered a week ago turned up. Only half of the children who had to go on Sunday, in fact, left the town.'[2]

Evacuees from Sunderland were billeted elsewhere in County Durham (some for instance went to Murton) or in the North and East Ridings of Yorkshire. Of their time away, Peter Hepplewhite comments: 'Although press reports painted a determinedly cheerful picture the reality was mixed. At best evacuees had their horizons widened and were treated

1 *Sunderland Echo,* 20 June, 1941, p. 4.

2 *Sunderland Echo,* 12 September, 1939, p. 2.

with great kindness.... Unfortunately not everyone was able to look back on a pleasant experience. The influx of city children was viewed by some in the country as little better than an invasion, and their resentment focussed on the evacuees thrust among them.'[1]

Indeed, evacuees soon started to return. This trend gained momentum and by Saturday 17 February 1940 about half of the 8,000 or so children who had been evacuated from the town at the start of the war were back at home. Consequently, the vast majority of Sunderland's children were present when bombs started to fall later in the year.

A popular advert of the period

Many of the evacuees returned to Wearside when Sunderland's schools were closed, a state of affairs that had existed since the start of the war, partly because the Board of Education would not allow schools to open in danger zones, a stance it maintained for a couple of months. Consequently, as a result of pressure from parents, from Monday 16 October 1939 onward the Local Education Authority began to hold classes for children aged nine or over in private houses and other suitable locations. This development was welcome news for some youngsters. For example, a girl told a reporter that, having become bored with inactivity hitherto, she had given lessons of her own: 'Daddy

1 P. Hepplewhite, 'The Home Front 1939-1945', in G.E. Milburn and S.T. Miller (eds.), *Sunderland, River, Town & People: A History from the 1780's to the Present Day*, 1988, p. 187 & p. 190.

made me a blackboard like the one at school, and I had ten infants who live in our street for my class. They were learning their ABC, and easy sums.'[1]

Shortly thereafter, on Monday, 6 November, Sunderland Education Authority reopened the Havelock School, which lay in a part of the town outside the evacuation area. Consequently, around 1,200 children from Ford Estate and neighbouring districts resumed lessons—the premises had been provided with suitable shelter trench accommodation in the event of an air raid. It was not, though, until early January 1940 that other schools began to reopen—including ones in the 'danger zone'—a process that continued into the spring. Schools could only open their doors once again after adequate shelter accommodation had been provided.

At the start of the war a nationwide blackout was introduced to hinder air raids. Sadly, though, many accidental deaths ensued throughout the country. One of those who died on Wearside was a 50-year-old sergeant major from Hull. He was killed at Queen's Parade, Seaburn, on Tuesday, 19 September 1939, for during the blackout he stepped in front of a bus from Whitburn that had just passed the junction with Dykelands Road. In all, there were 25 fatalities on the town's roads in 1939; 14 of which occurred after the start of the war and 11 of these happened during the blackout. The blackout remained in force in subsequent years but from early 1945, by which time the enemy were staring defeat in the face, street lighting was reintroduced in some parts of the town.

Sunderland experienced its first air raid in 1940. Shortly before noon on Friday, 9 August 1940, a solitary German plane dropped bombs on Deptford and the vicinity of Monkwearmouth Station. Four workmen were thus killed at Laing's shipyard, and 19-year-old Irene Mooney (of 86 Maplewood Avenue, Marley Potts) received injuries from which she died a few days later in Monkwearmouth Hospital.

Numerous other raids ensued and inevitably added to the toll of death and destruction. On the night of 3/4 May 1941, for example, bombs wrought havoc in Brandling Street and Westcott Terrace (now part of Brandling Street). One of those affected was Robert Moore, a retired

---

1 *Sunderland Echo*, 16 October 1939, p. 3.

Atkinson Road after a visit from the Luftwaffe

policeman, who was on firewatch duty near his house, 5 Westcott Terrace. During a lull in the raid, he decided to return to his house to have a cup of coffee and see how his wife, Margaret, aged 72, and 37-year-old daughter Elizabeth, were coping. As he approached his home another bomb fell and he 'saw the debris thrown into the air. Getting nearer I saw it was my own house and I realised what had happened to my home and my family. My wife and daughter I knew were sheltering under the stairs. They would have no chance at all. They must have been killed outright.'[1] Their neighbours, Mary Hannah Harvey, aged 34, and her two-year-old daughter Anne were also killed at the same address.

Sunderland's two worst raids of the war happened in the spring of 1943. On Sunday, 16 May, parachute mines, high explosive bombs and hundreds of incendiaries caused widespread death and destruction and

1 *Sunderland Echo*, Monday, 5 May 1941, p. 4.

Advert extolling the virtues of keeping fit—thanks to Eno's

claimed 70 lives. Furthermore, Sunderland's deadliest raid quickly followed, early on the morning of Monday, 24 May. In all, 83 people died and over 100 were seriously hurt. Among those who perished were 16 people in a brick and concrete shelter at Lodge Terrace, Hendon, destroyed by a direct hit at 3.15am. Thankfully, the raid proved to be the last Sunderland's residents had to endure—for Wearside the war from the air was over.

Turning to other matters, on Tuesday 17 October 1939 the *Sunderland Echo* reported that all activities along the town's seafront had ceased and would remain so for the duration of the war. In the event, although the beaches were mined and sealed off with barbed wire for most of the war, they were not completely out of bounds for the entire conflict. For one thing, the *Sunderland Echo* of Monday, 25 March 1940, notes that bathers had taken to the sea at Seaburn and that children were having horseback lessons on the sands. The same report also states that the promenades at Roker and Seaburn were thronged and that the hotels along the seafront were very busy. In addition, for the bank holiday weekend in August 1944 (several weeks after allied troops had landed in Normandy) the beaches were temporarily reopened. They became permanently available to the public in March 1945.

One of the ways the conflict made its presence felt was through rationing. Some of the commodities rationed included clothes, soap and paper. Food rationing, moreover, started on Monday, 8 January 1940, with butter, bacon or ham each rationed at 4 ounces, and sugar 12 ounces, per person a week. Allowances were later reduced and more commodities were rationed.

When the war began places of entertainment were closed nationwide because of the fear of air raids. However, this policy was soon abandoned. On Friday 15 September 1939 the *Sunderland Echo* reported that cinemas and other venues could reopen between 10am and 10pm. Several cinemas, including the Havelock, Marina and Regent, promptly resumed business on the same day whereas the town's most prestigious cinema, Black's Regal in Holmeside, did so the following day with a western entitled *Stagecoach* whose cast included a youthful John Wayne. Shortly thereafter, on Monday, 6 November, opening time for cinemas etc. was extended to 11pm. From mid April 1944 cinemas were permitted to open on Sundays as well.

Films shown during the war included *Casablanca,* starring Humphrey Bogart and Ingrid Bergmen, which was screened at the Ritz in Holmeside from Monday 5 July, to Saturday 17 July 1943. Moreover, on Monday, 20 March 1944 *Lassie Come Home* began a one-week run at the Ritz. Of the film a reviewer commented: 'The picture is in technicolour and some of the scenes are art studies in themselves. A picture that will satisfy every member of the family.'[1]

For its part, the Empire Theatre reopened on Monday, 18 September 1939, and over the course of the war attracted a wide range of artists, including comedians and visiting opera and ballet companies. Among well received performances of classical music were those staged in early December 1943, of which we read: 'Houses at the Empire Theatre have been almost capacity at each performance of the National Philharmonic Orchestra, and the quality of the guest artists has contributed in no small measure to the musical interest of this week; which it is hoped will be repeated at not too distant date.'[2] At least one patron, however, was not impressed with the behaviour of fellow members of the audience. He deplored the fact that some of those present had hummed along with

---

1 *Sunderland Echo*, 21 March 1944, p. 3.

2 *Sunderland Echo*, Saturday, 11 December 1943, p. 3.

the music or used loud passages of the music as opportunities to talk: 'There are others who do not even wait for such passages but converse at an even tone throughout. May I recommend them to the circus.'[1]

Thankfully, the war finally ended in 1945. Sunderland had certainly been more badly affected by the conflict than most other towns in Britain. For one thing, more people were killed by air raids here than anywhere else in the North East. According to figures given by the Town Clerk to the Imperial War Graves Commission in 1947, civilian deaths totalled 267, while 29 Civil Defence personnel had also died, all but one of them on duty. In fact, Sunderland ranked among the seven most heavily bombed towns and cities in Britain. For years to come, some areas of the town thus bore the scars of conflict. Emotional wounds, of course, endured long after rebuilding work had been undertaken.

---

1 *Sunderlanc Echo*, Thursday, 9 December 1943, p. 2.

ADVENTURES AT HOME & ABROAD — THE EXPLOITS OF DAVE DODDS

On Tuesday, 31 May 1955, an exhausting race was held in South Africa. Ninety-two athletes competed but many failed to reach the finish for the race was the gruelling Comrades Marathon, run between the cities of Durban and Pietermaritzburg, a distance of approximately 54 miles.

Dave Dodds, one of the contestants, was a 25-year-old Wearsider who had settled in Southern Rhodesia—today's Zimbabwe—the previous year. Dave, who had already come second in the South African marathon championships, ran well in what proved one of the fastest Comrades Marathons in the then history of the race. Indeed, he finished fourth with a time of 6 hours, 25 minutes and 15 seconds—less than 20 minutes behind the victor—and won the novice trophy given to the most successful first time entrant. Of the race he declared: 'The down-hills bothered me more than the uphills. At one stage my legs were jarred so badly I wondered whether I would finish.'[1]

David John Dodds was born in Sunderland on 20 January 1930. He came into the world in Millum Terrace, Monkwearmouth, a neighbourhood on the north side of the River Wear whose most venerable building, St Peter's Church, dates from the mid 670s. His parents had married at the church on 26 September 1927, and he was duly baptised there.

He was born into a family resident on Wearside since at least the late 18th century. His father, Thomas Walton Bulmer Dodds (1895-1980), was in the Merchant Navy and belonged to a family well known as river pilots. It was, for instance, the occupation of Tom's father, grandfather and great-grandfather, the last of whom had first been licensed to serve as a pilot in the early 1830s.[2]

---

1 M. Alexander, *The Comrades Marathon Story*, 1985, p.149.

2 According to the *Sunderland Pilotage Commission Register of Pilots* (held by Tyne and Wear Archives Service), David John Dodds (1803-78) was 5ft 9in tall and of fair complexion. He gained his first pilot's licence on 5 July 1833 and became a master pilot. The son of a Wear keelman, he married Dinah Tindle (1809-87) at St Hilda's Church in South Shields on 29 August 1831. At the time of his death he was resident at 38 Millum Terrace, his home for a number of years.

Dave's mother, Bella—christened Hannah Isabella Elliott Swinhoe at Holy Trinity Church in Sunderland's East End in December 1897—likewise came from a family with a local seafaring background. Indeed, at an early age she lost her father Benjamin (1851-1904), the captain of a Sunderland tugboat, the *Earl of Dumfries*, who was killed when the vessel blew up a mile or so off Seaham Harbour.

Although much of Monkwearmouth was blighted by squalor, Millum Terrace was more salubrious for it lay on the eastern fringe of the neighbourhood and overlooked the harbour. Dave Dodds' first years were spent living upstairs at 29 Millum Terrace, and of the place he recalls:

> As was the case in many homes at that time, there was no separate kitchen, and in the living room, meals were prepared, then cooked either on the coal fire, on a small gas burner, or both. The food was eaten, the dishes were washed in an enamel bowl, and on Friday, according to the local tradition of having a weekly bath, it became the bathroom. This ritual took place in a galvanised bathtub, which during the rest of the week hung from a nail on the backyard wall.

His paternal grandparents, David John Dodds (1868-1940) and Annie (née Bulmer), who married at St Peter's Church on 22 October 1891, also lived in the same street.[1] They did so at no. 33, a more substantial property with a wider and more elegant stairway that had a large landing from where his grandfather, a tall, autocratic figure, used to gaze out to sea with his telescope. Although certainly not a member of Sunderland's elite, as a pilot (his name first appeared in the Pilot Register in 1891) he was nevertheless a respected figure in the seafaring community in which pilots were a cut above the norm and earned significantly more than the average Wearsider. This point was noted in an article in the *Sunderland Echo* of 31 March 1932. The paper states that another pilot (a relative bearing the popular family name of David John Dodds) was involved in a legal dispute over payments to his estranged wife, and had earned around £360 the previous year, a weekly average of £7.[2] In contrast, few working-class males in Sunderland earned £4 a week.

1 Dave's grandfather was the son of Robert Tindle Dodds (1843-1928), who received his first pilot's licence on 18 April 1863. He was 5ft. 11in. tall and of fair complexion. In 1867, he married Hannah Foster, who had been born in Ireland.

2 The David John Dodds in question had lived at 35 Bede Street for many years before separating from his wife, who continued to reside at that address.

Dave's mother with an elder sister

In addition to visiting his paternal grandparents at Millum Terrace, young Dave Dodds enjoyed trips with his devoted mother, a petite, refined and affectionate woman of gentle disposition. Some of his happiest times with her involved crossing the river by ferry from Monkwearmouth to the East End. They would then stroll up Bodlewell Lane en route to the Old Market (which dated from 1830 and linked High Street East with Coronation Street) where a wide range of items could be bought.

On such occasions, they sometimes returned home by walking across Wearmouth Bridge—erected in the late 1920s—and from where they would look down at the activity on the river and its banks. For example, Dave recalls that a short distance downstream on the south side of the river was 'Austin's floating pontoon, on which would be a ship lifted totally out of the water, with workmen performing their various tasks to keep the vessel ship-shape.' They also enjoyed frequenting local parks and travelling by bus and ferry to Whitley Bay. There were also many happy times when his father returned from the sea and the house rang with laughter.

When aged five, Dave became a pupil at Redby School, which had opened on 1 December 1899 and lay beside Fulwell Road. Shortly thereafter, his parents left Millum Terrace and moved to 5 Whickham Street, likewise in Monkwearmouth. Of the move, he states: 'We lived downstairs, and another family lived upstairs. It was not only a more modern house, but it was spacious and... I was quite pleased with the move. It was also nice to be living directly opposite to stables, and I greatly enjoyed going across the road to feed the ponies with pieces of bread.' In the event, a few months later the family of three moved to live upstairs in a house near the top of Roker Avenue. Another change of address promptly followed, however. In the summer of 1935 they began sharing a recently built semi-detached house, 126 Newcastle Road. In addition to having electric lighting, other advantages of the new house were an indoor lavatory, a proper bath, tap water and a garden. The other occupants were his father's sister, namely 26-year-old Aunt Lex and her husband Wilf Brown, although the latter, an engineer in the Merchant Navy, was thus often absent for long periods.

Dave was delighted with the move but his happiness proved short-lived. His beloved mother, held in very high esteem by members of the family, fell ill and soon died on Thursday, 6 February 1936, aged 38. She did so in Monkwearmouth and Southwick Hospital, which had been founded in Roker Avenue in 1873 but had moved to more substantial purpose-built premises on Newcastle Road in 1932. She was buried in Mere Knolls Cemetery on the afternoon of Monday 10th February.

Following his mother's death, he continued to live at 126 Newcastle Road and to attend Redby School. Against his will, though, he was soon enrolled at a nearer school, namely Grange Park, erected on Swan Street in the early 1930s. But the change was not a success and he soon returned to Redby where he continued to be a pupil even after moving with Lex etc. to a house in Rosedale Terrace, Fulwell.

A significant event occurred in September 1937 when his father remarried. The bride, Rosalind Routledge, was an usherette at the Roker Cinema (which dated from 1915 and was near the Wheatsheaf) and the marriage took place at Holy Trinity, a church built in Southwick in the early 1840s. Thereafter, following a brief stay in Roker, the family moved to the ground floor of 11 Fitzroy Terrace, Southwick. The new residence comprised two main rooms, plus a small bedroom, kitchenette and bathroom.

Dave Dodds was subsequently enrolled at High Southwick School, which had opened beside Thompson Road in 1877 and lay several minutes' walk from Fitzroy Terrace. An avid reader, with a strong interest in history, he also spent many happy hours in Southwick Library, which lay slightly closer to hand. The library dated from 1931 and had been constructed shortly after Southwick became part of Sunderland, a change of status not welcomed by all of Southwick's residents. Pleasure was also derived from attending the Savoy, a cinema which had first opened its doors in 1912 and fronted Southwick Green. Uniquely among the town's cinemas, the Savoy projected films from behind the screen.

Roaming the local countryside was also great fun. At this time, land to the west of Burntland Avenue was undeveloped—a lane, partly lined by a hedgerow, led through fields towards the mining village of Castletown—and Dave played in Hylton Dene. Moreover, he sometimes ventured beyond Castletown to the hamlet of North Hylton and the wooded banks of the River Wear. Furthermore, in 1938 he enjoyed a holiday in upper Weardale where his paternal grandmother annually hired a cottage near Ireshopeburn.

A major change occurred in 1939. Days after the outbreak of World War Two, Dave boarded a train and was evacuated from Sunderland to

The Savoy Cinema

Kirby Wiske near Thirsk in Yorkshire—the final part of the journey was by bus. At Kirby Wiske, he was billeted on a farm and soon received word from his stepmother that the Sunderland-built collier, the *Goodwood,* of which his father was a crew member, had been sunk on 10 September after hitting a mine off Flamborough Head. The vessel, en route from the Tyne to Bayonne, was the first North East collier lost during the war. Fortunately, Tom Dodds survived almost unscathed in contrast to the captain, Harold Hewson of 9 Humbledon Park, Sunderland, who was badly injured and only returned to Wearside after spending a few months in hospital.

At Kirby Wiske, Dave was chided in a letter written by his stepmother, who took him to task for not responding to the news of the sinking of the *Goodwood*. He replied on 21 September, stating:

> Dear Mam and Dad I am very sorry that I did not say I was sorry about my dad and the ship. I received your letter and parcel. Thank-you very much for the comics .... I am in very very bad need of wellingtons. I am glad John Sloan [a fellow Southwick evacuee] went home. It is nice feeding the hens. I am better off than you, we have a car.
>
> With heaps of love from David, XXXX
>
> Good morning

On the whole, Dave enjoyed life as an evacuee and loved exploring the countryside. In addition, he attended school lessons at Kirby Wiske with fellow evacuees and local children.

Nevertheless, in common with many of Sunderland's evacuees, by the beginning of 1940 he had returned home. Several months later he attended the funeral of his paternal grandfather who died that June and was interred in Mere Knolls Cemetery; his widow was duly also buried in the same grave in July 1942.

In line with instructions from the government, at the start of the war schools in Sunderland had closed and this was still true of High Southwick School when Dave returned from Yorkshire. However, on Monday, 11 March 1940, lessons finally resumed at High Southwick, where his schooling continued until he progressed to Monkwearmouth Central

School in Swan Street, which had reopened on Monday 8 April 1940 and was adjacent to Grange Park School.

Sunderland was subjected to air raids from August 1940 onward and Southwick was one of the areas where bombs fell. The worst incident occurred late on Tuesday, 30 September 1941, when seven people (including five members of the same family) were killed at the corner of Shakespeare Street and Cato Street.

During raids, in addition to taking shelter, Dave sometimes eagerly scanned the skies. Indeed, while standing in Fitzroy Terrace he caught sight of an enemy bomber illuminated by searchlights. Anti-aircraft batteries soon opened up and the Heinkel began to disintegrate, sending the aircrew to their graves. He also recalls that he and his schoolmates used to collect shrapnel: 'In the playground, we would proudly show off our treasure, and swap pieces with the other boys. Usually, they were fairly small fragments, but one day I found the battered nose cap of an anti-aircraft shell, and this raised my status as I proudly showed it to my schoolmates.'

Apart from going on holiday in upper Weardale in the summer of 1941 (where he witnessed the crash landing of a Canadian plane whose pilot survived), Dave spent the remainder of the war on Wearside. And during this period one of his relatives, 59-year-old Frederick Dodds, a Wear pilot who lived in Roker, was fatally injured on the evening of Friday, 7 November 1941, when he was crushed between two vessels as he was attempting to board a ship about to enter the harbour.[1]

Subsequently, on Monday 7 May 1945, by which time Dave was working at the fitting out quay of J.L. Thompson's (a shipyard based at North Sands in Monkwearmouth[2]), fighting in Europe ceased. Like many of his neighbours, he celebrated VE day by enjoying a party and bonfire on vacant ground at the bottom of Alice Street—close to his home in Fitzroy Terrace—an occasion when housewives brought out

1 Frederick Dodds was born on 10 October 1882 and married Beatrice Wynne Williams at All Saints Church, Monkwearmouth, in 1906. During the First World War, he captained vessels for a shipping company based at Cardiff. Two of his sons became pilots and a third son died at sea. One of Frederick's grandchildren, Brian Dodds (b.1940), became Mayor of Sunderland in May 2000.

2 The shipyard was named after Joseph Lowes Thompson (1824-93), whose father, Robert, had founded the yard in 1846.

anything combustible, including furniture that appeared to be in reasonable condition.

Less than a year later, on Wednesday 23 January 1946, he began an apprenticeship at John Lynn & Company Ltd, an engineering firm founded in 1879 and based at Pallion, a part of Sunderland located across the River Wear from Southwick. He was taught to become a fitter and turner—making equipment including ships' winches and steering gears—but the training received was not particularly thorough and he states that the apprentices 'were a form of cheap labour.' Moreover, the 'factory was a ghastly place to work in. The windows, which were set high up in the wall, were never cleaned and some of them were broken' and much 'of the machinery was vintage and well worn, with little regard being paid to the regulations, which said that all machinery should have safety guards.' Nonetheless, 'the workmen certainly knew their trade.' During his apprenticeship, in an accident while working on the night shift, Dave lost two of the fingers on his left hand.

In this period, his interest in athletics began. One evening, in order to watch training in progress, he accompanied some of his workmates to the TLF (the J.L.Thompson, James Laing and Sunderland Forge Welfare and Sports Ground) that had opened beside Fulwell Road on 12 December 1922 with the 'hearty support' of Sir James Marr who was, among other things, the managing director and chairman of J.L. Thompson and Sons. Now occupied by the Fairlands housing estate, the TLF covered around five acres and had previously served as a clay pit and dumping ground. Work on transforming it into a sporting facility had taken about two years and had included draining a large pond and levelling the land. When the site opened the ground had provision for cricket and football. It was hoped to provide a running track as well. In the event, this had not occurred and races were simply run on the grass.

Upon visiting the TLF, Dave was promptly bitten by the athletics bug. Hence he frequently returned to train and proceeded to take part in a number of races. Shortly thereafter, he won a race in Newcastle and joined Heaton Harriers Athletics Club on Tyneside. In addition, he continued to run at the TLF and won several events in the summer of 1949. A more ambitious fixture, the famous Morpeth to Newcastle Road

Race (first run in 1904) also featured in his calendar and he finished in 11th place on Monday, 1 January 1951.

A few weeks later, on Tuesday 23 January, he completed his five-year apprenticeship at John Lynn's, whereupon he continued to work at the factory as a journeyman fitter. However, soon afterwards, on Friday, 9 February 1951, he left to begin his National Service and was given a company reference stating that his 'conduct and ability have given entire satisfaction.'

He was sent to Catterick Camp in Yorkshire but was discharged after only a couple of weeks or so when an officer spotted that two of his fingers were missing. He was thus deemed unsuitable for military service.

Soon after returning home, Dave joined the Merchant Navy. From Tuesday, 6 March 1951, he worked as fifth engineer on the *Avistone* and his first voyage was from North Shields to Narvik in Norway. The ship left Smith's Dock without a cargo but took on iron ore in the Scandinavian port before crossing the Atlantic to Baltimore. However, his days on the high seas proved brief for on Saturday, 14 July 1951 (after another voyage to the United States and one to Finland), he left the *Avistone* when it berthed in Middlesbrough. This decision elicited a jocular remark from his father that he had 'gone out on one wave and come back on the next.'[1]

A month later, on Monday 20 August, Dodds gained a position at Edison and Swan Electric Company's Cosmos Works at Pallion. The factory was located in a part of Sunderland where Joseph Wilson Swan, whose inventions included the incandescent light bulb, had been born in 1828.

Of his new place of employment, he says:

> I was amazed at how different the working conditions were compared with Lynn's. The factory was very bright. It had an inexpensive canteen, central heating, clean toilets, wash basins and changing rooms. Tea or coffee was brought around on a trolley mid-morning and afternoon, *and*, out of the staff of about sixteen hundred, only four hundred were of them were male.[2]

---

1 A reference from the ship's chief engineer comments: 'I found him to be willing and obliging, of good character, and at all times strictly sober.'

2 To begin with, Dodds worked in a department making and processing components for radio valves; from July 1952 he held the post of working chargehand in the Spray, Branding and Salvage Department.

A studio photo taken in 1948

National Service at Catterick Camp

With fellow engineers on board the *Avistone*

Some of the workforce comprised an athletics team and as 1951 drew to a close, Dave Dodds ran on a crisp winter's day in the Edison Swan cross-country championship in Essex and won the event.

By now he had developed a passion for opera, having been captivated by the film *The Great Caruso*, starring Mario Lanza, which he had seen at one of Sunderland's leading cinemas, the Ritz. The cinema, which had opened in Holmeside in 1937, had begun a week run of the film on Monday, 1 October 1951, but it proved so popular with Wearside filmgoers that it ran for another fortnight. Enthralled by what he saw and heard, Dave promptly began to collect records on opera, especially ones featuring tenors. He also attended a performance of Bizet's *Carmen* at the Sunderland Empire. Usually, though, he had to travel to Newcastle if he wished to see opera.

On Tuesday 1 January 1952, in inclement weather, he participated again in the Morpeth to Newcastle race and finished with a time of just over 1hr. 16min. He also represented Edison Swan at various athletics events, including races held in London and Manchester, and did so again the following year.

Furthermore, on Monday 9 June 1952, he participated (as a Heaton Harrier) in the Sunderland Police Sports Mile. Of the event, held at the Ashbrooke Sports Ground—a venue dating from 1887—he recalls: 'It was a handicap race, and my mark meant that to win it, I would have to pass a lot of runners, some of whom were starting more than fifty yards ahead of me.' Nevertheless, he won the race, watched by just over 9,000 spectators, and was presented with a silver tea service valued at £6, a sum that exceeded his weekly wage by £1.

In the same year, Dave developed a passion for motorbikes and purchased a second-hand Douglas 80 from a young Sunderland businessman, Tom Cowie, who had recently opened a motorbike showroom at Matamba Terrace, Millfield. Dodds, who had a competent command of German, also accompanied several friends on a motorbike tour of Europe, which included visiting Austria, Germany and Italy and he repeated much of the journey in the summer of 1953.

His attention was also engaged by another interest, chiropody. He enrolled on a correspondence course with the School of Surgical Chiropody based in Leatherhead, successfully completed the course, and was granted a certificate in 1953. Although he wanted to leave home and hoped to set up in practice in Sunderland, he encountered opposition from his parents and the scheme came to nothing.

In the same year, he swopped his Douglas 80 motorbike for a Royal Enfield Meteor 700cc and became a founder member of the Edison Swan Motorcycle Club. On Thursday nights, during the autumn and winter of 1953-4, he met at the Royal Hotel on Bridge Street with fellow members and, over a meal and drinks, planned journeys for the following Sunday: 'We would agree on the destination, the time and meeting place would be arranged, *and go we would*, hail, rain or shine.'

In early 1954, Dave Dodds got the urge to broaden his horizons further. Consequently, to the regret of his parents, after reading a job advertisement in the *Sunderland Echo* for the assistant work's manager at a factory in Africa, he decided to emigrate to Salisbury in Southern Rhodesia.

Hence on Tuesday 6 April, he left Edison Swan's and, at Easter, was given a lift to Newcastle where he boarded a train bound for London, from where he was to continue the rest of the journey by plane. En route, the aircraft refuelled at various destinations (including Malta, Egypt and Kenya) and the friendly pilot proceeded to veer slightly off course so that his passengers could have a breathtaking view of Africa's highest mountain, Kilimanjaro, as they flew over Tanzania. Finally, the plane landed in the city of Salisbury which was founded in 1890 and is now named Harare, the capital of Zimbabwe.

Dave was fascinated by his new surroundings and loved the climate. On the other hand, he was less impressed with the job that had brought him to the country. As a result, he soon began working for the Irrigation Department instead, a post that took him deep into the 'bush' where he and his colleagues carried rifles for protection from wild animals. He continued to work for the department until 1955 when he joined Central African Airways.

Meanwhile, within a week of arrival in Rhodesia, he became involved in the local athletics scene and soon broke the national marathon record, with a winning time of 2hrs 42min. Furthermore, in addition to taking part in other races in Southern Africa, he later finished seventh in a race from Marathon to Athens in October 1957, and represented the Federation of Rhodesia and Nayasaland at the British Empire and Commonwealth Games at Cardiff in 1958 where, owing to ill health, he ran a poor time.

Soon after returning to Rhodesia, Dave became an amateur jockey. He had been fascinated by horseracing since his youth. Indeed, while still in Sunderland he had hoped to become an apprentice jockey at Middleham in Yorkshire but his father had hidden a favourable reply from one of the trainers based there. Now, Dave took to riding in earnest. In fact he duly won 50 races, including the Rhodesian Grand National in 1965 when he rode *Templehof*, owned by a genial baronet, Sir Henry Grattan-Bellew, with whom he struck up an enduring friendship.

The last 11-mile leg of the 110-mile Gwelo to Bulawayo Long Distance Relay

The wedding day in Filabusi

By now Dave Dodds was no longer single, for on Saturday 4 February 1961 he had married 22-year-old Natalie Wright Crampton who shared his devotion to opera and was a classically trained pianist and singer. Although born in South Africa, where her family had settled in the mid 19th century, she had lived in Rhodesia since New Year's Day 1956, and was a member of staff at the Salisbury Academy of Music.

The wedding, however, took place at a village called Filabusi—over 300 miles from Salisbury—near to a farm owned by the bride's parents who had also moved to Rhodesia. A month or so later, the couple began their honeymoon. They flew to Europe where they visited several fascinating places, including Rome, Venice, Vienna, Paris and Berlin. The holiday ended with a two-week stay in Sunderland where the newly-weds lived with Dave's parents at a house the latter had bought in Enid Avenue, Fulwell. In addition to showing his bride around Sunderland, where much had changed since his departure in 1954 (for example, trams no longer plied the roads and ferries had ceased to cross the Wear) they explored the region's heritage and travelled up to Edinburgh.

Three years after getting married, Dave began a new career. He enlisted for ten years in the Royal Rhodesian Airforce and in 1965 the airforce dropped the appellation 'Royal' when, under the leadership of Ian Smith, the country broke away from indirect British rule, a move Dodds viewed with mixed feelings.

In his spare time during this period, he took up karate, which he pursued with characteristic determination. Indeed, in early 1968 he flew to England with his eldest son, Shaun, and obtained a brown belt

Shaun at the launch of the Greek bulk carrier *G.M. Livanos*

after being put through his paces by a Japanese instructor in London. On the same trip, he also travelled to Sunderland to visit his parents and introduce them to their grandson. Shipbuilding was still a major facet of the town's economy—the number of yards had however been reduced by closure or amalgamation—and in April, accompanied by his father and son, he witnessed the launching of the *G.M. Livanos*, a bulk carrier built at North Sands, Monkwearmouth.[1]

Six years later, Dave's days in Rhodesia came to an end. They did so in May 1974. The country had been subjected to growing insecurity since 1966. Black nationalists, one of whose leaders was Robert Mugabe, were engaging in an armed struggle with the aim of ending white minority rule, a conflict that had entered a more acute phase in 1972. This fact, combined with requests from his ageing parents for him to return, resulted in his decision to leave the country. Accompanied by

1 Since 1961 J.L. Thompson's shipyard at North Sands had been part of a conglomerate formed that year, namely, the Doxford and Sunderland Shipbuilding and Engineering Company. The largest vessels built on the Wear were constructed at North Sands.

Dave enjoying fishing at Lake McIlwaine near Salisbury in the late 1960s

his wife and three sons, Shaun, Glen and Gavin, he journeyed by train to Cape Town in South Africa, boarded a liner named the *Edinburgh Castle*, and sailed for Southampton, homeward bound.

Dave Dodds lives in Sunderland and his autobiography, *Running Shoes to Racing Silks – a Wearsider's action-packed life* was published in 2009.

STRIKING THE RIGHT NOTE — THE STORY OF SUNDERLAND PIANOFORTE SOCIETY

At 7.15 on the evening of Tuesday, 5 February 2013, one of the world's finest pianists, William Fong, entered the Pottery Room of Sunderland Museum and sat down at a magnificent Steinway concert grand piano. He then proceeded to delight the audience with music by Beethoven, Chopin, Schubert and Ravel. The event was a significant one for it marked the 70th anniversary of the Sunderland Pianoforte Society, a jewel in Wearside's crown.

The society was formed on 2 February 1943 as the Second World War was raging and in such dark days the formation of the society must have given some cheer to locals who loved classical music. The aim of the founders was to 'encourage the study and playing of piano music by presenting at least four concerts in each season.'

One of the founder members was Ted Ducker, who recalled that the decision to form the society was made by a group of friends who had previously met at a private home to listen to each other play the piano.

The fledgling society faced stiff competition, however, for concerts were held on a frequent basis at Sunderland Museum and Art Gallery under the aegis of the Council for the Encouragement of Music and Arts, which attracted highly regarded classical musicians to the town. For example, on the afternoon of Saturday, 25 September 1943, Kendall Taylor (Professor of Piano at the Royal College of Music) gave a recital at the Art Gallery.

Nevertheless, the pianoforte society struck a favourable chord with Wearsiders, a point duly noted by the local paper:

> Sunderland Pianoforte Society has completed a successful first season. Its third recital, held last night in the Girls' High School, followed the annual meeting.... Guest artist for the recital was Mr Karl Livock, whose virile playing of works by Bach, Scarlatti, Chopin, and Liszt was much enjoyed. Especially brilliant were

his renderings of Chopin's great Ballade in G minor, and Liszt's Hungarian Rhapsody no. 6.[1]

Although Sunderland Girls' High School (a private school founded in 1884) was the usual location for recitals in the early years, the venue sometimes changed. For instance, the society's sixth recital was held on Wednesday, 19 April 1944, at the Art Gallery in Sunderland Museum and the guest pianist was Iris Loveridge. In addition, four members of the society also performed at the concert, including an 8-year-old named Ruth Robinson.

The norm in the early years was to have part of the programme at each concert delivered by members of the society, whereas the rest of the music was played by a professional classical soloist. Subsequently, though, it was decided to introduce an annual 'Members' Evening' where all the performances were by members who had notified the society's secretary that they wished to take part.

A central figure in the society's history was Ronald Smith, a leading concert pianist who made his Proms debut in 1942. On Tuesday, 15 December 1953, for example, he performed at the concert hall of Sunderland Training College at Bede Tower and the programme included 'Scarbo' from Ravel's challenging work, *Gaspard de la Nuit* as well as music by Bach and Chopin. Of the performance, the *Sunderland Echo* commented that 'Mr Smith is never dull or casual. There is a subtlety of shading, an infinite variety of tone-colour about his playing .... This was one of Sunderland Pianoforte Society's most successful recitals.'[2]

Another noteworthy concert was held on Tuesday, 29 October 1957, when the recitalist was the highly acclaimed Eileen Joyce, a petite and eye-catching Australian-born musician who enjoyed celebrity status, having becoming exceptionally popular during the war years. Unusually, the concert was held at Seaburn Hall, a venue that had opened on Sunderland's seafront in 1939. For the occasion, the hall was packed and of the concert we read:

Eileen Joyce ... last night gave Sunderland Pianoforte Society one of the most successful recitals for several years .... Miss Joyce's playing

---

1 *Sunderland Echo*, Friday, 17 September 1943, p. 5.

2 *Sunderland Echo*,16 December 1953, p. 2. Smith had previously performed for the society during the 1952-3 season. He made several more appearances for the society: the last was during the 1981-2 season.

> is always full of interest ... for she brings out unfailingly the content and character of the music with warm-hearted sincerity, conviction and a finely controlled technique, and last night had the audience's rapt attention from the first gracefully moulded phrases of Beethoven's *Fur Elise* with which she began.

The review also notes that her programme included more music by Beethoven, as well as material by other composers. Although one of the movements of a work by Chopin was 'punctuated by bronchial interruptions from one of the people in the hall' the reviewer nonetheless concluded: 'Sunderland Pianoforte Society scored a resounding success with this recital.'[1]

At this date the society's piano was an old Bechstein—in the early days pianos had been hired or borrowed—but by the late 1950s, as membership was expanding, the decision was made to buy a replacement piano. Fundraising ensued and Ted Ducker subsequently visited several piano showrooms in London. He was accompanied by Ronald Smith, who tried out a number of instruments on the society's behalf. Consequently, on Smith's recommendation, in late 1960 a Steinway model D concert grand in a walnut Louis XVI style case was bought.

Smith himself was the first musician to use the excellent piano (one of a handful of that model made in Hamburg in the early 1900s) for one of the society's recitals. He did so at Bede Tower on Wednesday, 28 September 1960. Of the event, we read: 'It was a great success—a large audience and a wonderful recital—Ronald Smith, who has delighted audiences on his previous visits, was an ideal choice to give the season a brilliant start, and he excelled himself last night.'[2]

One of the pianists who has performed for the society more recently is Sarah Beth Briggs who was born in Newcastle upon Tyne in 1972. A prodigious talent, she first performed for the society during the 1983-4 season and the event was her first full-length evening recital. Sarah, who was subsequently joint winner at the International Mozart Competition at Salzburg, has returned to Sunderland on several occasions and her most recent performance for the society was well-received

1 *Sunderland Echo*, 30 October 1957, p. 2.

2 *Sunderland Echo*, 29 September 1960, p. 3.

Viv McLean

on Tuesday, 16 October 2012. The concert was held in the Pottery Room of Sunderland Museum, as has been the case with other recitals since the interior of the museum was given a thorough overhaul at the beginning of the century.

In recent years the pianist who has given the most recitals for the society is Viv McLean, a young Englishman who won first prize at an international piano competition held in Barcelona in 2002. For instance, on Tuesday 7 April 2015 he gave a spell-binding performance of music by George Gershwin; an event at which, unusually, the music was interspersed by an account of Gershwin's life narrated by the actress Susan Porrett, who thus contributed to the memorable occasion. It was a fitting finale to the 2014-15 season.

Details of forthcoming concerts can be found on the society's website. Tickets are available at the door and cost £12.50. Students and the unemployed can obtain tickets for £6 and recitals are free to children under 16.

Of Related Interest

A History of Sunderland – Third Edition

Glen Lyndon Dodds

Hardback 320pp; also available on Amazon Kindle.

'There was a real need for a scholarly, readable, overall history of the city from its origins.... What immediately meets the eye in Sunderland is not greatly stimulating to the historian (St Peter's apart) but... serious delving... begins to reveal considerable historical interest. It is excellent to have this interest brought out as vividly and attractively as... [this] book achieves.' Geoffrey Milburn, former Senior Lecturer in History, Sunderland Polytechnic.

'The accessible style... and the clear lay-out will appeal to an audience which requires a reliable summary of the history of one of Britain's newest cities.' Professor Richard N. Bailey.

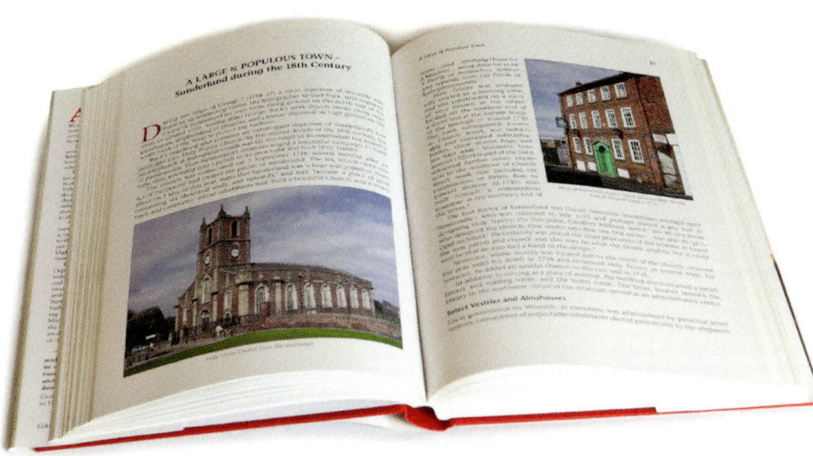

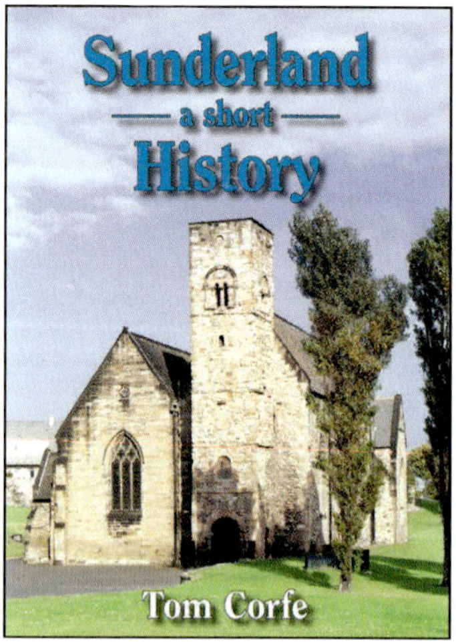

Sunderland—A Short History

Tom Corfe

Available on Amazon Kindle.

'...a compact but nevertheless comprehensive and fascinating account.... Attractively presented, well-planned and interestingly written with judiciously chosen illustrations and clear maps and diagrams.' *Durham County Local History Bulletin*.

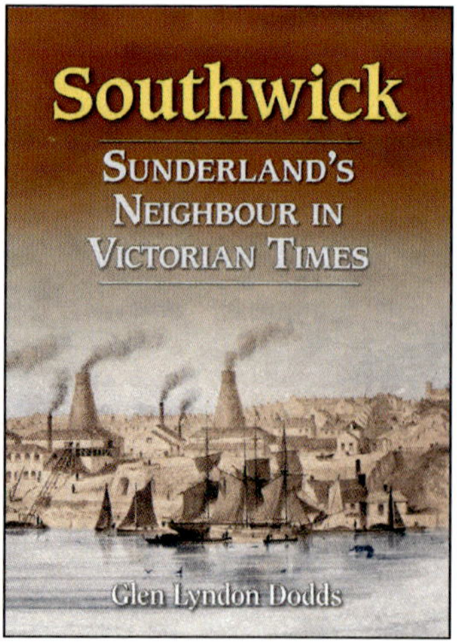

Southwick—Sunderland's Neighbour in Victorian Times

Glen Lyndon Dodds

Softback 32pp; also available on Amazon Kindle.

This attractive and highly readable work will appeal to anyone interested in Southwick's fascinating past. The reliable text outlines Southwick's history during a remarkable period and is accompanied by carefully chosen illustrations.